TRUSSVILLE PUBLIC LIBRARY
201 PARKWAY DRIVE
TRUSSVILLE, AL 35173
(205) 655-2022

"If you've ever been told to 'be more strategic' and wondered how to do it, this is the book for you."

—**Marshall Goldsmith**, *New York Times* #1 bestselling author of ***Triggers***

Be More Strategic in Business

How to Win through Stronger Leadership and Smarter Decisions

Diana Thomas & Stacey Boyle

Foreword by **Stephen M.R. Covey**

Be More Strategic in Business

Praise for *Be More Strategic in Business*

If you've ever been told to "be more strategic" and wondered how to do it, this is the book for you.

—Marshall Goldsmith, *New York Times* #1 bestselling author of *Triggers* and *What Got You Here Won't Get You There*

This is the book that you've been searching for if you need to take your strategic leadership to the next level. Thomas and Boyle pare down an overwhelming process into six factors for making smart decisions and showing other leaders that you are a strategic peer. Even seasoned leaders will find gems of wisdom from two women who've built successful careers and are eager to share what they've learned.

—Jan Fields, Former President, McDonald's USA; on *Forbes*' "World's 100 Most Powerful Women" and *Fortune*'s "50 Most Powerful Women in Business" lists

Being more strategic is really about what it takes to be more effective and efficient, leading yourself and others to places you have never been before. Diana and Stacey are correct that this quest is an ongoing journey, which begins with exploring your inner territory before venturing out into the field. Their framework nicely blends the hard and soft skills (quantitative and qualitative) required to move beyond tactics, considering the essential question of "why?" The book comes alive through sharing their own personal journeys (especially hard lessons learned through mistakes), along with many practical illustrations and highlighted action steps.

—Barry Z. Posner, PhD; Michael J. Accolti, S.J. Chair; Professor of Leadership, Leavey School of Business, Santa Clara University; and co-author of *The Leadership Challenge*

At a time when diversity of leadership is becoming a highly sought-after asset in the most powerful organizations, Thomas and Boyle give you the guide book to building your ladder of success. It doesn't matter where you are today—this book will get you where you want to be tomorrow.

—Rosina Racioppi, President and CEO, WOMEN Unlimited

I'm more strategic and successful for having been coached by Diana and Stacey, so I was delighted to find lots of great personal examples throughout the book. The content lays out a clear path that will help any business leader learn how to strategically build out a plan for success with chapter takeaways and checklists that guide the process step by step, or rung by rung.

—Alexandra Mustafa, Training Leader, Penske Motor Group

In the book *Be More Strategic in Business*, the authors have created an excellent treatise of leadership behaviors to improve business outcomes. There are useable, actionable nuggets of information for leaders to employ right away.

—Jack Groppel, PhD; Cofounder, Johnson & Johnson Human Performance Institute, and Author, *The Corporate Athlete*

In times of constant and accelerated change, the ways way we conduct business continue to evolve, but the need for strategic leadership will never go away. Thomas and Boyle are the coaches you need in your quest to become a top leader in your organization. Embrace the principles outlined in this book and bring strategic leadership to your organization today!

—Jeanne C. Meister, Partner, Future Workplace and Co-author *The Future Workplace Experience*

Connecting investments and meaningful business results is a challenge for many critical business functions. The Impact Blueprint provided by Thomas and Boyle is a powerful tool for aligning to the business and driving meaningful change.

—Karen Kocher, Global General Manager, 21st Century Jobs, Skills and Employability, Microsoft

By sharing the wisdom gained in their own successful careers as business leaders, Thomas and Boyle have created a practical guide for anyone who has been told they need to be more strategic.

—Dennis Kennedy, Founder & Chair, National Diversity Council

Be More Strategic in Business is packed with reminders, questions for reflection, and actionable advice from two leaders who have built their reputations on connecting to the business and driving winning results.

—Gary Whitney, VP, Global Learning, Intercontinental Hotels Group

This book demystifies the process of showing the outcomes of investments using a simple, practical tool, which we have successfully used to communicate with stakeholders and donors. However, it goes further than that, pulling together the many skill sets needed to successfully lead a thriving organization.

—James Collins, Director, Learning and Advocacy at Greater Twin Cities United Way

Leadership is both art and science, a combination of inspiring vision and relentless execution. In *Be More Strategic in Business*, Thomas and Boyle provide a compelling, modern leadership model that resonates in today's rapidly changing world of work. If you're ready to take the next step in your career, this book is an invaluable roadmap to your leadership journey.

—John Taggart, CEO, Human Capital Media, Publishers of *Chief Learning Officer and Workforce*

If you can't look and act strategic, you'll be fighting an uphill battle to accomplish your business and career goals. *Be More Strategic in Business* gives you a framework for a leadership journey that will lead to long-term success.

—Anna Wildermuth, CIM, ACC Founder and President of Personal Images, Inc.

We tell leaders all the time to be results-oriented while also driving the management team from a shared vision of the strategic plan. Thomas and Boyle show you how to make a smart plan, and then shift into action so you can deliver!

—Kray Kibler, CPA, MBA; CEO of Scrip Companies

Be More Strategic in Business

How to Win Through Stronger Leadership and Smarter Decisions

Diana Thomas & Stacey Boyle

Mango Publishing
Coral Gables

Copyright © 2018 Diana Thomas and Stacey Boyle
Published by Mango Publishing Group, a division of Mango Media Inc.

Cover Design: Roberto Nunez
Layout Design: Jermaine Lau

Mango is an active supporter of authors' rights to free speech and artistic expression in their books. The purpose of copyright is to encourage authors to produce exceptional works that enrich our culture and our open society. Uploading or distributing photos, scans or any content from this book without prior permission is theft of the author's intellectual property. Please honor the author's work as you would your own. Thank you in advance for respecting our authors' rights.

For permission requests, please contact the publisher at:

Mango Publishing Group
2850 Douglas Road, 3rd Floor
Coral Gables, FL 33134 USA
info@mango.bz

For special orders, quantity sales, course adoptions and corporate sales, please email the publisher at sales@mango.bz. For trade and wholesale sales, please contact Ingram Publisher Services at customer.service@ingramcontent.com or +1.800.509.4887.

Be More Strategic in Business: How to Win through Stronger Leadership and Smarter Decisions
Library of Congress Cataloging
ISBN: (print) 978-1-63353-784-2 (ebook) 978-1-63353-785-9
Library of Congress Control Number: 2018944498
BISAC category code: BUS063000 — BUSINESS & ECONOMICS / Strategic Planning

Printed in the United States of America

Dedication

Diana

I dedicate this book to all of you leaders who persevered when you realized you needed to be more strategic, especially those who have trusted me to be their coach.

Stacey

I dedicate this book to a future strategic leader and my precious peach, Emma. You are the inspiration behind everything I accomplish in life and give me astronomical pride and hope.

Contents

Foreword

If your goal is to become a powerful leader who fulfills her or his purpose, you will love this book.

I was honored when Diana Thomas—a long-time student, facilitator, partner, and friend of the FranklinCovey team—asked if she could use a leadership analogy she heard from my late father, Dr. Stephen R. Covey, as the basis for a new strategic leadership model. When I found out Diana was going to turn that model into a leadership book she was coauthoring with Stacey Boyle, I became very intrigued by what they were up to.

Diana is a highly sought-after visionary and strategic leadership coach; Stacey is an expert in analytics and evaluation, helping companies move the needle on important business measures. While they're both accomplished professionals on their own, their unique partnership has the potential to teach strategic leadership in a way that's practical and contextualized in today's business environment—something that you don't often find in leadership books.

As I sat down to read their manuscript, I was struck by just how applicable the book would be for anybody who is coming into a leadership role. Diana and Stacey are giving you the complete picture here—everything from the personal attributes you need to help others perceive you as strategic to the time and prioritization techniques we have taught in our organization to the ways that leaders plan, execute, and show critical results.

What this powerful pair has done in this book is similar to what I've attempted to do with the principles that underlie trust. Just as I've sought to help people see that trust is not merely a soft, social virtue, but rather a hard, economic driver that can be learned, Diana and Stacey have taken the vague, elusive advice of "be strategic" and made it into a practical, actionable set of skills that can become habits.

This isn't just a book for new leaders. There are many leaders who have been managing organizations for some time, others who perhaps have been passed over for promotions, and still others who are struggling to think strategically and connect their function's activities to what matters most to the business. The latter have not developed what I call "TASKS"—the Talents, Attitudes, Skills,

Knowledge, and Style to strategically affect people and results. Having spent much of my career working with leaders in the human resources space, I know they have unique challenges—and opportunities—when it comes to driving business results. Diana and Stacey grew up in that world, and what they share in this book is all the more valuable because it's been time-tested in one of the more difficult disciplines to lead strategically.

Core to my father's and my personal leadership philosophies has been the importance of being strategic—of leaning your ladder against the right wall of success in work and life. This analogy used in *Be More Strategic in Business* is the backbone of what the authors identify as the six factors for strategic leadership. These factors are essential for anyone who needs to be more strategic in organizational contexts—public and private companies, non-profits, government, small business owners, entrepreneurs, and start-up founders. That's because, no matter what type of organization you're working in, you need to be able to look across the landscape of your jungle and ensure you're focused on the things that will get the results your organization wants and needs to see.

In my work helping leaders and organizations build trust, I've noticed that the lack of trust costs individuals and organizations dearly—what I call "Trust Taxes." Similarly, if you are too tactical in your approach to understanding your business' needs and providing solutions, your influence and career will be taxed or limited. Conversely, there are "Trust Dividends" that are earned when you wisely extend trust, increase your credibility, and behave in ways that inspire trust with your stakeholders. So it is that there are significant benefits when you intentionally choose to be strategic in your work of leadership and influence.

I'm confident you will enjoy both the destination and the journey of becoming more strategic, and that developing this competency will increase your credibility and results as a leader. This wonderful book will show you how.

Stephen M. R. Covey
Author of *The New York Times* and #1 *Wall Street Journal* bestseller *The Speed of Trust*; former President & CEO, Covey Leadership Center

Introduction

When we first met each other, back in 2010, we had no idea that the needs driving our initial meeting would eventually turn into a process for you, our leader-reader, to cultivate your own strategic leadership capabilities and then apply that skill set throughout your organization. No, we got together under the premise that one of us had a missing piece and the other knew how to fill in the gap but lacked a platform for sharing her knowledge. Our relationship grew over the years as we helped each other in many ways, and eventually we realized that putting our skill sets together created a combination that is desperately needed in the business world.

We want you to know where we come from because our individual stories are the genesis of our model. Most of the book contains our collective wisdom, but occasionally we'll share specific insights that come from one of us. We want to give you our wins, lessons learned, mistakes, and occasional embarrassments so you can turn them into your opportunity to excel.

Stacey

Ouch.

That was my initial reaction to my first performance review in my first professional job after earning my PhD at the age of twenty-nine. I was used to being the sharp and successful girl in academia, so it was pretty shocking to find out that I was too detail-oriented and that people didn't like meeting with me, among other things. Where was this feedback coming from, and what the heck could I do to change it?

It took several years, many interactions with seasoned leaders, and an intense amount of work in the field for me to get to the bottom of what my bosses were telling me—that I needed to be more strategic. That's a phrase that's thrown around in a lot of employee review meetings and frequently goes unexplained. The recipient walks away with a vague feeling of something to work on but without a practical plan for acquiring a so-called strategic skill set. I loved research, digging into numbers, creating spreadsheets, and mastering the details of everything I worked on. I couldn't understand how "too detail-oriented" had suddenly become a bad thing!

I watched my Andersen Consulting (now Accenture) colleagues gain promotions while I was passed over. I was told to be more strategic, but I really had no idea what that meant, what I was doing wrong, or where to go to learn how to become a strategic contributor. Frankly, my bosses weren't equipped to help me. I was firing off spreadsheets full of complex calculations while they were asking for straightforward answers to their questions. Right out of academia, I didn't yet understand how to distill my research findings into meaningful answers to management's strategic questions. In the high-pressure environment of Andersen, where everybody was smart, successful, and competitive, I really couldn't afford to flounder.

After a couple of years, I moved on and directed my career more specifically into the corporate training field. During this time, I realized that I loved the consulting model. It gave me the ability to dig into the details that energized my work, but at the same time I was able to be out in the world, working with dynamic individuals and tackling new problems in a variety of industries. Human capital analytics became my niche. The problem was, in the early 2000s, no one in the market knew what that was, and no one in the nascent field had figured out how to package it in a way that was mainstream and palatable to the potential customers who stood to benefit.

In the fall of 2005, I arrived late to a Chief Learning Officer conference. I rushed into a ballroom and stood at the back, only to find that the keynote speaker had already begun her talk. It so happened that this was Diana's first keynote; she had been invited to speak at a time when McDonald's was transforming from a struggling fast-food restaurant chain to a thriving corporation. I wasn't sure who Diana was, but I was quickly captivated by the talk and said to myself, *I want to work with this woman!* I could see that Diana had the vision and drive to run a successful learning department. Diana seemed to realize something many learning leaders at the time didn't grasp: that she needed to communicate with her stakeholders (in this case, executive leaders and franchisees) in a way that spoke to their business needs. However, when I saw the results she presented, I realized just how much McDonald's could benefit from being able to show a true link between investments on the learning side and results in the restaurants.

After the talk, Diana was mobbed with people wanting to meet her, and I hung back. I knew I could help Diana, but I also knew that my ideas would be well over her head at this point in time. No one in the learning space was making meaningful connections between their learning data and business data. If these kinds of results were shared at all, they were loose correlations. Diana had shown how HR investments had seemed to lead to a rise in sales in the restaurants, but she couldn't get specific about what training had done to drive those results.

About five years later, I joined *Chief Learning Officer Magazine* (*CLO*), the organizer of the conference where I had seen Diana's presentation. My role at *CLO* was to create an awards program for enterprise-class learning programs. Applications evaluating nearly every aspect of a learning leader's function were judged by leading practitioners in the learning and development industry. Winners were ranked in an annual list known as the LearningElite. The program quickly grew in popularity, and soon Diana's team at McDonald's applied. Nearly all of the learning departments at this time were doing little to evaluate the effectiveness of training, and those who were evaluating were making workforce learning and development decisions based on departmental data and learner surveys. No one was exploring predictive or causal models (that is, what could happen as a result of a key decision). A subset of those departments were estimating a financial return on learning investments.

At this time, the winds of change were beginning to blow ever harder in the learning industry. With the rising popularity and affordability of technology, as well as the 2008/2009 recession, corporate learning and development had gone from delivering classroom training and paper manuals to e-learning and on-demand content. The next iteration of that change was a growing attempt to become more precise in showing how learning impacted the business in meaningful ways. The term predictive analytics was gaining traction in other disciplines (marketing, supply chain analysis, etc.), and there was a small-but-growing faction of thought leaders who were finding ways to apply predictive analytics to employee development investments. It was expensive, took a long time, and was confusing to the majority of the industry. But it was creeping into the lexicon. Software vendors were organizing and pitching new platforms to simplify people data.

Against that landscape, I began to think about ways to push the industry toward showing more business-oriented results on their LearningElite applications. I wanted to see a learning function showing data-driven links between dollars invested in learning and results that were important to the business. Gradually, companies like Accenture, Lowe's, and the U.S. government reported that they were using quantitative and qualitative data to go beyond reporting on training's status. These organizations were assessing training's impact on the bottom line and employing predictive analytics to make strategic decisions. Even smaller businesses were starting to leverage data and use advanced analytics to make organizational decisions. At CLO, we began offering consulting packages to entrants. We would take an award application, and then put together some recommendations based on the organization's current state benchmarked against other similar organizations and feedback from LearningElite judges to propose a consulting engagement with the company. Remembering Diana's 2005 presentation, I made a pitch to McDonald's and received a first meeting with Diana. At the time, Diana had a vision for what measurement could do for Hamburger University, but she didn't know how to bring it to life. She had brought in consultants and software vendors, but the market for learning evaluation was so immature at the time that she hadn't been able to achieve her vision of showing the business how learning investments drove sales in the restaurants. She and I began to collaborate, and the rest, well, you'll learn in this book!

Today, I run my own consulting firm. I help other organizations harness their people data and make smarter decisions. My firm also has a strong presence in the not-for-profit arena, showing how investments in communities foster long-term growth and success.

Diana

I launched my career with McDonald's Corporation as a sixteen-year-old crew member in a Maryland restaurant. My job there was hostess, which meant I was supposed to greet customers and interact with them while they were in the restaurant. Initially intimidated, I soon learned how to talk to customers. Little did I know how important this would be throughout my career, as meeting the needs of customers became a critical touchstone at every major point of decision. As I entered college, I began climbing through the ranks at my restaurant. Shortly before I graduated from college, I completed a career assessment, which told me I was well suited for human resources. I inquired about opportunities with McDonald's and was granted an internship in Washington, D.C., that led to a long-term role recruiting crew and managers, as well as partnering with colleges on career programs.

Although I was one of the younger leaders working in that D.C. regional office, I was rarely intimidated. I'd been blessed with tremendously supportive parents who had raised me to believe I could do anything I set my mind to, and also that you can't get something if you're afraid to ask for it. I was working under successful leaders and on the lookout for ways to learn from them (and actually learning even more from a few weaker leaders). I had a chance to attend a series of talks by motivational speakers with our leadership team. Two that have stood out in my mind over the years were those by Zig Ziglar and Joel Barker. I felt so inspired by their presence and the messages they delivered, and I was motivated to do whatever I needed to do to become the type of leader who could make people feel that way. In fact, my own leadership platform came from something Joel Barker said in one of these sessions: "An effective leader is someone who you will choose to follow to a place you would not go by yourself." I began to think more critically about my own personality and skills and how I could channel those into becoming the type of leader people would want to follow.

My next promotion landed me in the training department at

McDonald's, and I quickly fell in love with my new career direction. Growing up, I had always wanted to be a teacher, so training felt like a natural fit. I started working toward my master's degree, which culminated in a thesis on leadership. Truth be told, I had a long-standing fascination with the topic. In 2002, I was named dean of Illinois-based Hamburger University and also began studying for my MBA. Personality-wise, I knew that I tended toward big-picture thinking. I was never too detail-oriented and didn't enjoy working with data and analytics. I began learning how to channel my big-picture thinking into a strategic focus, and I also found a niche helping others around me grow from individual contributor to strategic leader. During this time, we began applying for the LearningElite, even though I felt pretty strongly that we weren't at the level of the winning organizations. I knew that showing proof of impact was a big gap. Our first entry earned us rank #42, and I looked at that benchmarking process as a chance to grow and improve.

In 2004, I completed my MBA, and shortly before that became vice president of training, learning, and development for McDonald's U.S. Around this time, feeling quite proud of all I had accomplished, I hosted a networking session at Hamburger University. Bill Wiggenhorn, then chief learning officer at Motorola, was one of the attendees, and it was the first time we met. We got into a conversation about growing and learning as a person, and what was on my mind was all that I had done to get to this point. Bill asked me how I was planning on staying current and abreast of the never-ending changes that would continue to impact learning organizations around the world. I was taken aback as he bluntly told me I would be dated within five years if I couldn't keep up—and he couldn't have been more right! Up to this point, I had succeeded largely though formal education and job training. Now that I was on the executive team, I needed to take my development into my own hands. Bill later became a long-term mentor for me, and I also added the role of learner to my own weekly compass. Bill helped me to see that it was essential to nurture my longtime love of learning by continuing to make it an essential, ongoing part of my work and life.

I first met Stacey via networking, as I was a member of the CLO editorial review board. When she came to McDonald's to talk to me about how we could improve on the weaknesses in our LearningElite application, I began to fully appreciate her combination of deep, analytical knowledge and the ability to highlight what was important from a strategic perspective. Stacey knew how to paint a picture of what data and analytics could do for McDonald's. I had been sharing business results with our franchisees, but I couldn't directly link those results to training. No one was asking me to do it, but I knew that day was coming and understood the importance of being able to back up my assertions with facts. Stacey helped to fill in the missing pieces and got us started on a journey at McDonald's. We began showing concrete results from training, taking baby steps at first (and a few wrong turns!), and it caught on like wildfire. Our stakeholders loved knowing that when they sent their people away for training, they could expect business results.

I retired from McDonald's in 2015. I've realized my lifelong dream of running my own business. Today I'm an executive coach, working with blossoming leaders to help them improve the things that are important to them, as well as helping them to find a healthy balance between their careers and their personal lives.

Our shared experience

One of the benefits of having grown up in the learning industry, and now through our own business pursuits, is that we have worked with leaders in almost every discipline and sector imaginable—from huge public companies, to smaller private organizations, nonprofits, schools, and government. In addition to our work with learning industry leaders, we've consulted with and coached leaders in human resources, IT, sales, marketing, new product development, federal agencies, and school district administrations.

And this is the beauty of the model we've created: no matter what field you're in, what type of organization you work for, there is a need for strategic leadership. You need to show your business how its investments are driving performance in the areas that matter. You need to be able to do that in a way that's enticing to other leadership. You need to unite your team around a motivating vision and help them understand how everything they do impacts the business in some way. You need to pull back from a reactive habit of spending your days putting out fires. You need a way to win people over to your cause. Whether the leaders you're working alongside are investors in your small, one-person shop; shareholders in a huge, multinational corporation; board members of a nonprofit organization; or the other leaders at the executive table—they are looking to you for strategic leadership, and this book is your guide to delivering on that need.

Chapter 1

Finding Your Ground Amidst Disruption

Your career is at a crossroads. You have the opportunity to lead. To win. To build something from the ground up and be successful. But first, you must make a great shift: from tactical, gets-stuff-done worker to strategic leader.

Have you ever been told you need to be more strategic? Or maybe you need to work on getting to the point, not presenting endless details, numbers, and facts, but distilling your case into a motivating vision. Your counterparts are moving up in the organization, and you can't figure out why you're not. Have you been passed over for a promotion because you fail to see the big picture? Are you starting your own business, knowing you need to set yourself up for success but unsure of how to go about it? If you're anything like us when we were on the receiving end of this feedback, you probably thought, what the heck does that even mean?!

Meanwhile, out in the world around you, everything keeps changing and evolving. Technology is replacing jobs traditionally thought of as human-only pursuits, and that's a scary thought. Simultaneously, technology creates the need for new skill sets, including many that are difficult to anticipate or prepare for. You may be just five years out of school and already need to update your own skills. Change has been a constant force in life for as long as humans have walked the earth, yet it continually surprises us. Think about this for a minute: twenty years ago, did anyone have the job title social media manager? What about SEO specialist, virtual assistant, UX designer, Uber driver, blogger, drone operator? This is just a small handful of positions created by changes in technology, and they in turn change the ways we live. Have you ever booked your vacation to stay in someone else's city apartment or ordered groceries using an app? These are things the vast majority of people weren't even thinking about twenty years ago. Now, we take such services for granted.

Think of reactions to change on a spectrum. At one end, you have those who cling to the old way of doing things. They say things like, "This is the way we've always done it," or "If it ain't broke, don't fix it." At the other end of the spectrum are the people who jump onto everything new and shiny. They're the ones who have to have the newest gadgets the day they come out and are never,

ever satisfied with business as usual. The majority of people fall somewhere in the middle of this spectrum, trying to grapple with all the changes around them and determine when to stick with the traditional methods and when to embrace the newest fad. These decisions aren't easy in your personal life, let alone when you're making them at the larger scale of a business.

And when it comes to business, the workforce is changing dramatically, too. Not only are some job functions becoming obsolete while others have a nearly insatiable demand for talent, but even the ways we think about the structure of a company are evolving.

> **Diana**
> When I started at McDonald's, it was common for an individual to climb the corporate ladder within one organization for the duration of his or her career, the way I did.

> **Stacey**
> My career journey of moving from company to company, doing independent consulting work, and eventually establishing my own firm is much more typical today.

Companies now have a mix of employees and contractors, contingent workers, and outsourced functions. They may exist across the globe, with coworkers who rarely or never meet in person. The dynamics of the worker-company relationship have changed so dramatically that it's ever more critical that you can show how you are impacting business performance.

And these are just sweeping, global changes. We haven't even gotten into industry-level changes—like disruptor companies, changing consumer needs and desires, economic issues, supply-side shortages…the list goes on. The way people learn has changed dramatically. In the past, if you wanted to learn something or answer a question, you had to find a library book or take a class. Today, you can google it or watch a video online. A big, important part of being a successful strategic leader is understanding all of these changes and—the magic ingredient—making smart decisions about how to manage them. Think back to that change spectrum. If you're on the far left, resistant to change, you will quickly become obsolete. If you're on the far right, you'll be endlessly distracted by every new trend that pops into your inbox.

You can be the hardest-working person in your company, but if nobody can see how what you're doing contributes to the bigger picture, then you'll continue to be passed over for promotions.

There's more to being strategic than managing change—a whole book's worth! In a nutshell, when someone tells you to "be more strategic," what they want is for you to show how you're driving corporate strategy and adding real value. Notice the word *show*. You can be the hardest-working person in your company, but if nobody can see *how* what you're doing contributes to the bigger picture, then you'll continue to be passed over for promotions. Now, if you're in sales, this may seem clear-cut. You have a quota, or you can show a dollar amount that you sold, which in turn helped your company to make money. But for every other discipline out there, it's less obvious. Maybe your job is to develop new products—how can you show that the products you're envisioning will be wins for your company? Or maybe you work in IT, which can feel like a cost center (or a necessary evil!). How can you show that what you do is helping to increase productivity across the organization? If you want to lead at the executive level, you certainly need to work hard. But you also need to get results, *and* you need to share those results in an enticing way.

In this book, you'll learn how to do two key things: first, how to show up and be perceived as a strategic leader. Second, you'll learn how to take your strategic behaviors and apply them through your organization for stronger results. We wrote this book for leaders and aspirational leaders who want to get to the next level. You're in a leadership role or will be soon, but you need to do something to improve and get to the next level. By improving your leadership and showing your results, you will get there.

What Happens When Strategic Leadership Is Missing?

It's often useful to define a concept by talking about what it's not. In an organization without strategic leadership, everyone stays in their own silo. People keep their heads down and get their jobs done without an understanding of why they're doing what they're doing. They may work extremely hard, but they're not intentionally applying their efforts to the things that will drive the company's desired outcomes. Waste is rampant as people fail to communicate across disciplines, and the wheel is frequently reinvented in multiple places. Layoffs feel random because the bosses don't know who is really contributing to business results. Meetings are long and unproductive as participants show up late and unprepared, and then bore each other to tears with irrelevant information. Pet projects receive undeserved attention while difficult change is overlooked because it's unpopular or too hard. Everyone chases the shiny, new, innovative decisions, to the detriment of what the organization does well.

We're going to give you two examples of publicized situations where strategic leadership was sorely lacking. When you're at the strategic level, your decisions are very often made on a public stage. When you make a mistake, there can be huge consequences.

Diana at McDonald's

In the early 2000s, McDonald's stock tanked. The company had just made several acquisitions of other restaurants that took the organization away from its core business of running a unified, well-loved brand experience. As a result of the acquisitions, McDonald's had lost focus on what we had previously done so well—that is, we lost focus on the McDonald's customer.

I was new to the home office at this time. In fact, I had been there a grand total of two weeks. The CEO, Jim Cantalupo, had retired but was brought back to save the company. His first order of business: meet with everybody in the home office who had recently come from the field. He wanted to know what was really going on out there. I nervously shared what I had so recently seen happening in the restaurants: they were dirty, quality had gone down, and we were not listening closely enough to customers. Crew members weren't even allowed to take orders from customers asking for a different condiment on a signature sandwich.

Cantalupo eventually turned McDonald's around by shedding the new acquisitions and focusing on what we could do well: listen to customers and provide an experience that would make the restaurants their favorite place to eat and drink. In this case, a strategic, big-picture view meant understanding that the company had gone too big with its strategic direction and reining in the innovation and growth until the core of the business could be strong again.

Whole Foods

Not long after Whole Foods was acquired by Amazon, customers began noticing empty shelves. A lot of empty shelves, actually. Photos of produce sections with only a stray lettuce leaf or onion peel trended on Twitter from customers in some of the largest markets in the U.S. Customers also complained publicly about rotten and rancid products and assumed Amazon was to blame. The problem, as it turned out, began before the Amazon acquisition.

Business Insider acquired a copy of a Whole Foods manual describing order-to-shelf (OTS), an inventory system designed to "help Whole Foods introduce more automation into its inventory management system by streamlining food buying and other store-level decisions."[1] The system appeared to have the opposite effect, along with a crushing impact on employee morale. In the past, store employees could fill holes

1 http://www.businessinsider.com/whole-foods-internal-documents-on-empty-shelves-2018-1

> on shelves with products they knew were strong sellers in their stores, keeping the shopping experience appealing. Under the new system, the manual instructed employees to leave holes empty, helping "ensure that OOS [out-of-stock] items get reordered because the hole is visible."[2] Furthermore, a point system penalized employees for any products that weren't in the proper shelf position, with the potential for department managers to lose their jobs over too many infractions.
>
> In many of the articles covering this story, employees are unnamed due to fear of being fired. In the past, Whole Foods has won accolades as a top employer due to its strong culture and valuing of even the lowest level employees. The order-to-shelf system is another example of a short-sighted decision from the top that wreaked havoc across the organization. By taking away the autonomy of its store employees, Whole Foods created a public relations disaster for itself. Time and again, we've seen examples of leaders who fail to value the employees throughout the organization, and as a result they inevitably see their share prices tumble.

What's the secret to strategic leadership? It's the ability to see the big picture and think through decisions in a way that connects to the right actions and gets the right results, taking the company where it needs to go. In spite of change all around, strategic leadership never loses its value.

Why You?

We wrote this book for the people we consult with, the people we coach, and even for the people who we ourselves were earlier in our careers: leaders who need to do something different to take themselves and their organizations to the next level. You may be a high-potential employee, used to succeeding and performing well. You want to win, you want to lead, and you want to drive real, measurable results in ways that matter. You're seeing other people around you succeed and be promoted while you stay in the same

---

2 Ibid.

What's the secret to strategic leadership? It's the ability to see the big picture and think through decisions in a way that connects to the right actions and gets the right results, taking the company where it needs to go.

place. What's the difference between them and you?

Some people are visionaries. They're fired up by new ideas, excel at having a macro point of view, and want to race ahead to implement a grand vision. Others are detail-oriented and love being in the weeds with specifics and data, working to understand the intimate details of how work gets done. The world needs both types of people. Strategic leaders harness elements of both personality types by becoming aware of their own strengths and then creating a personal development plan for gaps or looking to outside resources (collaborators, hiring new staff, etc.) to compensate.

The fact that you picked up this book means you know you want to evolve in some way. We can't underscore this point enough: if you want to be a strategic leader, you must be ready to change yourself, change your department, and change your organization. Willingness to change and improve underlies our entire model.

Imagine this: you are part of a team evaluating something in your organization that's high-profile, expensive, and beloved. Maybe it's a national advertising campaign, an employee productivity platform, a major training curriculum, or a sales channel partnership. Whatever it is, it's near and dear to your department and well-known throughout the organization. When the findings from the analysis begin to roll in, you find out that the program isn't working. You thought it was successful, but it turns out those success metrics aren't driving business results. You've just learned that you are pouring money into an initiative that's not doing what it's supposed to. What decision do you make? What are your options?

Reading this scenario in a generalized format, it's relatively easy to say, "Of course I'd pull the plug." But put yourself through the mental exercise of coming to such a finding about your flagship initiative. The one for which you personally pushed to get funding, and then promoted to everybody with lots of grand promises about a huge ROI. It's personal, and it's painful. It's so painful that those kinds of findings are often shelved. People make excuses: the evaluation model was flawed, or we didn't have access to the right data to prove the impact, or the political climate is such that we need to stay the course, or the CEO loves this program, so it has to stay.

Here is where we stop and tell you that if you aren't ready to cut your pet project after finding out that it's not delivering the value the company needs, then you aren't in the right mindset to read this book. Set it aside and come back when you're ready for blunt honesty, a truth that is sometimes agonizing but leads to better things. You can make a huge difference, but it all starts with your willingness to change in order to drive smart, organizational change. And sometimes willingness to change means we have to let go of the things we love. It means asking hard questions and running the risk of appearing foolish. It could mean you have to tell your boss that she made a critical mistake or confronting naysayers when you typically avoid conflict. It also means asking for help and advice from those around you, reaching out to connect with supporters and denigrators alike. Above all, willingness to change means being the kind of leader that your organization so desperately needs you to be.

What's All the Fuss about Change?

Driving change can be scary when you're acting alone. Throughout this book, you'll notice a common theme: pulling together all available resources to get the job done. Strategic leaders don't work alone in a silo—they connect with their colleagues around the organization in order to gain a systemic perspective on the business and ensure that they are meeting the needs of internal and external customers. Strategic leaders also make smart, informed decisions based on robust evidence that has come from all types of data. When it comes to thinking about and using data, many people get overwhelmed. It's easy to get lost in the sea of vendors, tools, techniques, databases, dashboards, scorecards, frameworks, and all the other options available for managing and interpreting data. But when it comes right down to it, using data is all about driving change in a focused, strategic way.

Data ▶ Information ▶ Intelligence ▶ Decisions ▶ Change

Figure 1.1

Evaluation and analytics take data and turn it into information. Information provides you with knowledge, which you can synthesize into intelligence using your experience and understanding of your organization. From there, you are equipped with what you need to make strategic decisions, which in turn drive change. Understanding the change you are trying to drive will inform all of your efforts. Decisions that require a change to something (a strategy, a system, people, a program, an investment, etc.) should be based on data. Evidence-based (i.e., data-rich) decisions result in change that improves outcomes, reduces risks, and optimizes investments.

You've probably heard about evidence-based medicine, which has only grown in popularity since it was introduced by Dr. David Sackett in the late 1970s. Evidence-based medicine is the "idea that decisions in medical care should be based on the latest and best knowledge of what actually works."[3] This is the same concept we apply to leadership in the business world—that leaders make decisions based on data. If you think this all sounds crazily obvious, consider this: "Studies show that only about 15% of [doctors'] decisions are evidence-based," which means that although there is a ton of medical research in existence, doctors aren't using it.[4] The same applies in organizations: we have absurd amounts of data, but instead we make decisions based on gut feelings and what someone else is excited about. One caveat: it's possible to go too far with data-driven decision-making, too. You always look at the big picture along with what your data is telling you. Strategic leaders use a combination of information to make smart decisions.

---

3 *https://hbr.org/2006/01/evidence-based-management*

4 Ibid.

The subject of using data brings us to the topic that we know makes many of you without a strong mathematics background cringe. It's okay. You aren't alone, and you don't need to revisit college statistics to become a strategic leader. No matter what area you work in, you have the opportunity to look at business results and determine whether you're doing the right things to get those business results. Some disciplines have a strong, obvious connection to business performance (sales, for example). For others, it's less obvious. A good example is the field we came out of: learning and development, or training. The learning department was traditionally considered a cost center because training the workforce was considered a cost of doing business. We knew we needed to train people so they could perform and we could stay competitive and innovate. But when times turned tough and the workforce dwindled, training seemed like a luxury. We could no longer take people away from their jobs to participate in training, and we didn't need as many people building and delivering training. This is not a strategic approach, because it stifles the competitive and innovative nature of business. However, it has, in the past, seemed like a sensible business decision on the surface due to a lack of proof that training was impacting the desired business results. So, why keep investing in something that may or may not be working? There was no clear evidence either way.

Because we came out of a field that struggled to connect its investments to revenue, we can confidently say that you can find a link between anything you're working on and the greater business strategy[5]. If a direct or indirect link truly doesn't exist, then you need to ask why you're doing it.

When it comes to analyzing data and showing business results, the answer is simple: if you don't already have a plan for evaluating your investments and decisions, you need one. That plan can be simple or robust, but it must be executable and help guide your strategic decision-making. Without understanding the impact of what you're doing, you're adrift. In your role, you may not need to have strong quantitative capabilities yourself, but business acumen and analytical awareness are critical leadership skills. Understanding

---

5 *How to Measure Anything: Finding the value of intangibles in business* Douglas W. Hubbard (2014)

analytics enables you to use data to drive change for winning results. Other leaders will take you seriously when they see that your decisions are fact-based and designed to move the company in the right direction. Leveraging all types of data when making decisions is a key component of strategic leadership, and it also empowers your organization by providing other leaders with data they need to build a truly competitive and innovative organization.

Leveraging all types of data when making decisions is a key component of strategic leadership.

You make decisions in life every day, some big and some not so big. Making an impulse purchase of a candy bar in a gas station is a decision that takes almost no thought. The cost is low, so even if you end up regretting the purchase, you aren't out much. Most people don't, on the other hand, buy an expensive sports car on impulse. You shop around, planning out where you're going to store it and how you're going to budget for all the higher ongoing costs of ownership—maintenance, tires, premium fuel, insurance, etc. In your own life, these details are usually easy to see and think through. As you get higher in an organization and have more responsibilities, you can't immediately see all the details yourself. This is why strategic leaders use data to monitor what's going on and make proactive changes when things aren't going the way they should.

How Do We Win?

A winning organization—whether it's a large corporation, a small mom-and-pop business, a start-up, a department, a team, or some other functional grouping—operates in alignment with the business. It has a vision and mission that are closely connected to corporate strategy, and everyone on the team is aligned to that vision. People on the team are enthusiastic about supporting the vision because they understand how their work connects to the organization's success. Who doesn't want to be part of a winning organization? The leader has an active, strategic role at the executive table and consistently steps back from everyday operations to evaluate everything the organization is doing. The leader makes sure all relevant stakeholders are informed, understand the desired impact, have their needs met, and play their part in enabling the organization to do its job. Further, everything a winning organization is doing is in some way making a needed impact on the greater business. When impact on the business misses the mark, the leader has the data necessary to identify the miss and moves quickly to remedy the situation. A winning organization's leaders are agile by evaluating what they're doing based on its impact on the business, making data-driven decisions, and making proactive efforts to change when change is warranted.

What's a Strategic Win?

A strategic win drives the company's performance in some fashion. To get specific, you and your organization need to decide what defines a strategic win. The important thing is to make those decisions at the outset, because you won't know you're winning if you haven't defined success in the first place. The Impact Blueprint™[6] presented later in this book will be a great help in defining success and identifying the big-picture macro wins, as well as the micro wins that tell you if you're making progress along the way.

Here are some examples of strategic wins.

Honeywell's response to economic recession

The traditional school of thought about recessions is to restructure the workforce, that is, lay people off. When business softened, Honeywell's CEO David Cote was reluctant to take this approach. He explains:

> To understand that reasoning, look at what really happens when you do layoffs. Each person laid off gets, on average, about six months' worth of severance pay and outplacement services. So in essence, it takes six months to start saving money. Recessions usually last 12 to 18 months, after which

6 Impact Blueprint is a trademark of Smarter People Planning, LLC

demand picks up, so it's pretty common for a company to have to start hiring people about a year or so after its big layoff, undoing the savings it began realizing just six months earlier.[7]

A winning organization's leaders are agile by evaluating what they're doing based on its impact on the business, making data-driven decisions, and making proactive efforts to change when change is warranted.

Instead of restructuring, Cote and his team implemented a series of unpaid furloughs. The organization worked through some heavy challenges during the furlough periods, but in the end the company emerged strong. Employee morale stayed higher than it would've under layoffs, and as business began to pick up, the skilled workers were ready to jump back in. Cote's leadership was strategic because he was able to see beyond the immediate pain of the recession. That, combined with some creative problem solving, put Honeywell ahead of its competitors when the economy was ready to grow again.

Educational assistance for employees

One strategic opportunity for McDonald's Corporation was the education support program, which had a rather low participation rate. The original design of the program aimed to give employees throughout the organization the opportunity to earn a four-year degree, which seemed to the team who launched it to be a useful benefit. When the team surveyed the audience eligible for the program to find out why they weren't taking advantage of the opportunity to get a four-year degree, they learned that the audience was still several steps away from that educational level. Many needed to complete a high school diploma or GED, and others felt that a two-year degree was more conducive to their goals. The team realized that the educational program would better serve this audience by offering pathways to a GED and/or two-year degree. Not only did they employ data to make this decision, but

7 https://hbr.org/2013/06/honeywells-ceo-on-how-he-avoided-layoffs

they asked the employees and partnered with outside organizations to find out how they had built their education strategies.

Improving workforce education levels also had the benefit of improving retention and strengthening the organizational leadership pipeline. Many employees were moving up through the ranks without a degree but eventually getting to a level where they needed additional knowledge and skills to meet the demands of the business world. Much of that was offered within the company, and the educational program helped to supplement internal training.

To continue winning and to employ the lessons learned from the tuition assistance program, the McDonald's team decided that they would gather more direct data on the front end to design and deliver the most beneficial program possible.

Leadership's pet project

A client's organization was spending millions on a sales training program with little to show for it. Sales numbers remained unchanged. The CEO was friends with the owner of the small training company that provided the sales program and thought it would be a big win for his company. The rest of the team, with no emotional attachment to the vendor, wanted to cut the program, but the CEO continued to fight for it. In these kinds of situations, hard data is so critical to getting your message across. You must be able to show results (or lack thereof) in business numbers. For the sales training program, the group (including the CEO) compromised by letting the sales training run for six more months. If at the end of that period results continued to be unchanged, they all agreed to cut the program. The metrics of success were clear to everyone involved, and they were able to detach from the personal factors involved.

Creating a winning organization requires strong, strategic leadership. Based on our experiences, both in and out of corporate L&D, we've developed a leadership model that is a microcosm of the six factors for strategic leadership you'll read about later in this book, and it will help you begin to think about the way winning organizations operate.

1. **Align with a motivating vision that's grounded in expectations.** Defining an inspirational vision is the critical first step in providing your team with the direction and motivation to achieve success. A sound vision provides everyone with a clear line of sight to the strategic win. This vision needs to be grounded in the definition of success for your company and business—based on customer and stakeholder expectations. We'll talk more about how to identify the company's strategy and success measures, as well as how to craft your vision, in later chapters. But as you define success, be sure to include what satisfaction looks like for your employees, customers, and shareholders (if applicable). Your vision should be a motivating statement—one that's tied to stakeholders and is a stretch for the organization. Everyone on the team should be able to relate to it, repeat it, confidently and enthusiastically explain it, and more importantly, live it! In fact, the vision statement should be incorporated into your daily language and interactions with others outside of the organization.

2. **Define goals and strategies as a road map to success.** Once you've crafted a motivating vision, define the key goals and strategies needed to bring your vision to life. These become the roadmap to your destination. Identify the critical actions that must be executed to move you along the right path. Leaders and team members should focus on actions that will have the greatest impact on desired results.

3. **Have the right players in the right roles.** To have the right players in the right roles, you start by hiring the right people. Staff for success by keeping your standards high and hiring the best. They don't necessarily have all the technical knowledge or fancy credentials, but the right disposition. Look for people who have the right attitude, willingness to be team members, and a desire to learn. Do they reflect the vision and mission for your organization? Are they the role models you want? Will they relate to the work and stick around to see the results? It's not only much easier to accomplish your goals when you

have strong players, it's downright impossible to accomplish them with weak players. Don't waste time and effort trying to improve the people who may be strong performers but don't have the right attitude or lack the willingness to learn. No matter how much time you sink into them, you can't force them to truly care about the job at hand or be a team player. Find the right fit for your team. Recruit, hire, train, and develop team players who have the ability and passion to bring your vision to life.

4. **Create the best work environment so everyone thrives; celebrate success!** Create an environment that allows people to not only do good work, but to thrive as they're doing it. Ensure workload is broken down into manageable chunks, and then match tasks and projects to the skills of each individual so they can accomplish their best work. People do their best work when they feel comfortable bringing their whole selves (mind, body, and spirit) to work. Take the time to get to know what motivates your team—what jazzes them. Most people have the sense that they work for a person, not for the company, so stay connected with them as individuals. Recognizing and celebrating successes is a strong motivator to keep team members productive and engaged. If you celebrate what you want to see more of, you'll get it! Ask yourself: "Would you want to report to or work with you?" What's good about reporting to you? What could be better?

Ask yourself: "Would you want to report to or work with you?"

5. **Plan, Do, Study, Act.** Winning leaders have a plan. They execute that plan. They learn what was revealed during the plan's execution, and then they act to make the informed change. Several later chapters will provide in-depth guidance to help you with strategic planning, execution, decision-making, and continual improvement.

6. **Measure functional success and focus on continuous improvement.** Item one entailed defining your vision of success. But to know if you're on track along the way—and if/when you achieve success—you need to measure your progress. Establishing regular check-in routines will give you and the team the opportunity to recognize and celebrate progress, which creates energy to keep going forward or make needed course corrections at the right times. These routines also provide the ideal opportunity for feedback—a tremendous gift when given and received in honesty and openness. Set ever higher goals to continually improve the business and to keep your stakeholders delighted.

People may not remember what you say, but they will remember how you make them feel.

Get Ready to Become a Winning Strategic Leader

You've probably heard the advice often given to leaders: people may not remember what you say, but they will remember how you make them feel. How do you want people in your organization to feel about you and your team? Your internal team wants a sense of purpose, an understanding of the connection between their work and the organization's larger picture. When you set your vision, ensure you are creating purposeful work. By helping your team see the way the vision aligns with corporate strategy, you help them see they are working for something bigger than checking items off some to-do list. This same model applies outside of your team, too. Speak frequently about your vision and help others in the company to know what you're doing and why you're doing it.

Next, we'd like to introduce you to two fictionalized leaders who will appear throughout this book. While they are a conglomeration of people and behaviors we've worked with and coached (and sometimes ourselves), any resemblance to real people is purely coincidental.

Taylor

Taylor is a tactical director at a medium-sized company. She excels at accommodating requests from everyone throughout the organization, and she manages her team so that they can quickly accomplish any work brought to them. Her team's direction shifts as the demand for learning ebbs and flows. She's a team player, works hard, and is hands-on with her team as much as possible. When invited to strategy meetings, she's always rushing in at least 5-10 minutes late and brings reams of data in complex spreadsheets. She tends to be long-winded when presenting to the executive board and likes to share her methods for analyzing the data because she thinks it helps her seem credible. Many board members fail to see the relevance of her points and question whether to invite her to future meetings. But she brings donuts from everyone's favorite local bakery, so it's hard to cut her from the invite list.

Sam

Sam is a strategic director at the same medium-sized company. She's focused on the big picture and is always thinking about a desirable and attainable future for the company. She's able to connect her vision with the company's vision, and her team understands their own direction. She also shares that vision with everyone she meets throughout the organization. Everyone knows what Sam's department is up to. Members of the executive board value Sam's input, and she's frequently included in strategy sessions. She comes equipped with data that shows how her department is impacting corporate goals. Less strategic leaders in the organization find her intimidating because of her constant focus on the big picture and avoid taking last-minute meetings with her when they don't have time for ample preparation. Sam is starting to earn a positive reputation in her industry for her thoughtful social media activity, blog posts, magazine contributions, and very popular conference sessions on driving winning results.

Sam and Taylor will help to illustrate the concepts presented in this book; look for them in the coming chapters and decide which archetype suits the needs of your organization.

To start, we will present Taylor and Sam in terms of leadership behaviors. As you learn more about Sam and Taylor, it's worth noting that we've all been Taylor in our careers! The majority of people start their careers in a tactical role, and then at some point need to make the shift to become strategic. Some people, in fact, prefer tactical roles, and that's okay! It does, however, mean that they aren't suited for strategic leadership. Sometimes we need characteristics of both (whether found within ourselves or by collaborating with others), but we need to know when it's the right time to unlock that skill set. As you go through the book, when you find yourself identifying with Taylor over Sam, it should trigger you to take a hard look at your role and what your business needs from you.

Strategic Leadership Behaviors

There are a number of competency models for high-level leaders; we offer a more informal list of traits and behaviors that have proven successful in our work and have been benchmarked against other leading organizations. The list below are skills that are most important for today's leaders of strategic organizations. As you look through these, consider the following:

- Where do you see areas for your own improvement?
- Do you see yourself acting like Taylor when you should be more like Sam?
- What are one or two things you could add to your own current development plan in order to get your journey started?

These core behaviors apply across any function. When you build your own development plan, don't forget to drill down into your own discipline for function-specific competencies.

1. **Plan and act strategically.** Develop a clear and compelling vision, strategy, or action plan that is aligned with your organization's goals and possesses a clear view of the future of the company. Having better industry and cultural knowledge

enables you to anticipate market and economic trends. Take a longer-term view of the business and the market, and translate the business strategy into meaningful goals and objectives for your department.

Strategic Sam behaviors

- Evaluates and pursues opportunities based on their fit with the broader organization
- Helps others understand how they impact measures of business performance and the organization's overall business success
- Creates a long-term vision for the organization that clearly defines how it will achieve maximum and sustainable competitive advantage
- Ensures business plans and investments consider future needs and global/industry trends
- Creates a solid plan, and then act upon that plan
- Makes informed decisions based on the best data available

Tactical Taylor behaviors

- Has little or no understanding of or interest in the vision/strategy of the business or of how individual or team goals connect to it
- Stays focused on their own initial objectives and priorities, even when the business circumstances change
- Spends excessive time on elements too tactical for her job level
- Does not keep apprised of industry trends and changes
- Is often seen as working in a silo
- Does not build professional networks across the organization
- Is excited to jump into doing without a clear plan or understanding of the purpose

2. **Customer and stakeholder focus and understanding.** Understand your customers' and stakeholders' needs, concerns, and problems. Strive to deliver high-quality products and superior services that exceed the expectations of your internal and external customers.

   Strategic Sam behaviors

   - Stays in touch and listens to internal and external customer feedback
   - Focuses the organization on maximizing key customer offerings and efforts that enhance loyalty and commitment
   - Enhances colleagues' understanding and appreciation of a diverse customer base
   - Monitors the external environment to identify long-term implications of change, e.g., the market or customer behavior

   Tactical Taylor behaviors

   - Does not approach issues with a customer-first mindset
   - Does not truly listen to her customers' and colleagues' needs
   - Reacts instinctively and jumps on a quick solution
   - Fail to recognize opportunities and the potential impact on the customer
   - Not taking time for customer and stakeholder contact
   - Assume that all customers' and stakeholders' needs are the same and/or cannot change

3. **Develop and lead engaged and committed teams.** Build a highly engaged and committed team. Leverage the skills and commitment of your team to accomplish stretch goals and objectives. Build and leverage your talent base by seeking out high performers, helping others develop and grow, rewarding high achievement, and supporting diversity of thought and perspective. Make your teams the most desirable place to work in the company.

Strategic Sam behaviors

- Holds self and others accountable for developing people
- Identifies and develops talent pools that reflect workforce demographics and business needs
- Creates an environment that retains talented people by addressing critical workplace issues, e.g., career development, work environment, and life balance
- Leverages diversity to drive superior performance
- Ensures that she and her direct reports have clear, specific performance objectives in writing

Tactical Taylor behaviors

- Overemphasizes proving oneself and fails to give credit to others
- Fails to give others constructive performance feedback
- Does not let go of tasks that should be accomplished by others
- Does not apply consistent criteria and standards when making decisions about the people on her team

4. **Lead through influence.** Positively influence others and collaborate in ways that inspire others to take action and/or change their perspectives.

Strategic Sam behaviors

- Creates new and uses existing coalitions to achieve organizational results
- Builds a broad base of support and influences key internal and external leaders
- Ensures leaders are motivating their employees with minimal reliance on authority
- Inspires passion and excitement in others by appealing to their values and goals
- Hires the best people who are motivated to support the vision

Tactical Taylor behaviors

- Often fails to get support for ideas and projects
- Fails to energize others
- Does not make others feel as though their point of view has been heard
- Is only able to get things accomplished through a directive leadership style
- Hires people who can be micromanaged so they will produce more work

5. **Lead change and innovation.** Identify the changing needs of customers, employees, and the system as a whole, and successfully lead innovation that improves the business.

   Strategic Sam behaviors

   - Champions ideas and best practices from both within and outside of the organization
   - Leads change in strategic directions for the organization in response to customer or system needs
   - Develops strategies for large-scale change initiatives
   - Creates a culture that fosters innovation

   Tactical Taylor behaviors

   - Stays fixed on how things have always been done
   - Resists new ideas
   - Avoids taking risks
   - Applies old solutions to new problems
   - Generates ideas that are not suitable for the needs of the business

6. **Continual learning.** Continual learning is an attribute that reflects your ability and willingness to change and gain from experiences and to apply learning effectively across diverse situations. Assess and recognize your own strengths and

opportunities and pursue self-development as needed. Leading research supports the understanding that learning orientation is an indicator of success in future leadership roles. This attribute adds a future focus to how we view an individual's potential.

Strategic Sam behaviors

- Quests for self-development
- Seeks and uses feedback from multiple sources (peers, customers, and subordinates)
- Engages in active listening with the intent to learn
- Asks questions in a way that shows a genuine curiosity and desire to learn
- Proactively advances knowledge and capabilities through a robust individual development plan
- Reflects on experiences and applies lessons to future experiences
- Adapts quickly and easily to new or changing conditions
- Identifies patterns/trends and apply them to new or unfamiliar situations
- Experiments with new ideas or approaches to determine what works best
- Brings out the best thinking in others
- Encourages others to experiment with new ideas and respectfully challenges others to think in unconventional or unprecedented ways
- Shares ideas and best practices with other parts of the organization to help strengthen the business

Tactical Taylor behaviors

- Reacts defensively to feedback
- Is unaware of her own development needs (has significant blind spots despite being given clear feedback)
- Demonstrates overconfidence in her knowledge or abilities
- Fails to apply information broadly or to new experiences
- Becomes overwhelmed by complexity or ambiguity
- Resists new ideas or approaches
- Prefers to think and act in standard ways, consistent with what has been done in the past

Quick and Dirty Takeaways from This Chapter

Are you ready to take your leadership to the next level? Here are a few things to remember from this chapter:

- **Change is a constant state of being, and it drives the need for strategic leadership.** Don't let yourself become obsolete in an ever-evolving world. Build your strategic leadership capabilities and show your organization how vital you are in achieving business results.
- **Don't be passed over for another promotion.** Get the missing pieces in place and take your leadership to the next level.
- **Smart decisions that drive change are rooted in data.** You need data to be synthesized into information that builds organizational intelligence in order to make strong decisions that drive winning results.
- **Winning leaders focus on the vision, themselves, and winning.** Start thinking about your personal development plan, and don't forget to develop your team, too. Make sure you understand the difference between strategic and tactical. We've all been tactical in our careers, but strategic leadership requires you to delegate the tactical elsewhere.

Chapter 2

Six Factors for Strategic Leadership

When executives tell you to be more strategic, they want you to see the big picture, not just of your department, but of the organization, industry, and market. The higher you move within an organization, the easier it becomes to see the big picture. You have conversations at a higher level and are privy to information that applies to the entire organization (versus a narrow focus on your specific area of responsibility). You also benefit from broader exposure to people who already think in a big-picture way. It can seem like a catch-22, because you can't get to the higher levels without looking and acting strategic, but it isn't always obvious how to get a big-picture understanding (let alone show executives you have that ability) without being a part of those executive circles. When you're starting out, the onus is on you to build up your strategic leadership capabilities. If you haven't heard it yet, don't wait for someone to tell you to be more strategic—desire to do that on your own.

Stephen R. Covey uses an analogy of producers cutting through a jungle to help explain leadership and big-picture thinking:

> Envision a group of producers cutting their way through the jungle with machetes. They're the producers, the problem solvers. They're cutting through the undergrowth, clearing it out. The managers are behind them, sharpening their machetes, writing policy and procedure manuals, holding muscle development programs, bringing in improved technologies, and setting up working schedules and compensation programs for machete wielders. The leader is the one who climbs the tallest tree, surveys the entire situation, and yells, "Wrong jungle!" But how do the busy, efficient producers and managers often respond? "Shut up! We're making progress."[8]

To be strategic, not only does the leader need to separate himself from the work of the producers and managers to climb the tree, but he also requires the courage to report back on his findings—that what everyone is busily working at below is in no way contributing to the expedition because they aren't even in the right jungle. And

8 https://leadershipforlife.wordpress.com/2011/08/23/hi/

then he requires more courage to stand up to the managers who say, "We're making progress!" Can't you just imagine Taylor, our tactical leader, standing on the jungle floor, surrounded by charts and graphs showing the number of plants felled per machete per day relative to the growing brawn of the cutters and sharpness of the tools? She's overflowing with evidence of progress! Unfortunately, Taylor's evidence is irrelevant in the wrong jungle. In this book, we are equipping you with the tools you need to build a ladder that will help you to thrive and continually win!

When Was the Last Time You Tried to Climb a Tree?

Whether it was last week, last decade, or a far-away time and place you can't easily recall, take our word for it: climbing trees isn't easy—regardless of whether it's a literal tree or the metaphorical tree in Covey's jungle. Our goal in this book is to show you how to build a ladder from the floor of the jungle to the treetops. By building a ladder, you have the ability to go up and down, using each rung as needed to help you make decisions and drive winning results. The ladder you build will be based on a time-tested model for strategic leadership applied to the modern business world and designed to address your unique needs, both as an individual and as a leader in your organization.

You will build each rung using our six factors for strategic leadership. We're going to take the messy, overwhelming process of becoming a strategic leader and giving you an orderly framework for setting and accomplishing goals, evaluating what you're doing, and improving on your results.

The Rungs of the Ladder

Below you'll find a summary of each factor, and the following chapters will go into greater detail to help you make use of each one. If you are only just learning about strategic leadership, you will find it helpful to read through each chapter for your strategic foundation. For those of you who are already doing some of these things, you may want to skip around and focus your attention on strengthening your weak areas.

Factor 1: Develop your foundational skills

Whether you're an aspiring leader or already in the role, you must create your own personal development plan. Factor one will give you everything you need to put that plan together. It's up to you to decide what you need to work on and determine those areas where you're already strong. Learning how to understand the big picture, see your place within it, manage your time, and show up in a strategic way will give you solid footing on the first rung on the ladder.

Factor 2: Establish the vision

Every action a winning leader takes is tied to a clear vision. You'll learn how to create a vision and strategy that are clearly linked to the corporate strategy.

Factor 3: Engage stakeholders

Establishing a governance board offers a structured way to bring stakeholders into your work. We'll explain how to identify your stakeholders and ensure you're delivering value to them, as well as how to foster shared accountability.

Factor 4: Build your strategic plan

A strategic plan is your blueprint for success. By starting with the end goals, you have a focused process for planning out the activities that will drive results. Our Impact Blueprint is the tool you will use to create a visual for what you're doing, where you're going, and how you will win.

Factor 5: Execute your strategic plan

You can't plan forever—at some point, you have to act, and you need to lead a great team to drive results while you're making sure you're still in the right jungle. When change, crisis, or confusion inevitably arises, you need to be prepared to act swiftly and get on the new track.

Factor 6: Make decisions to win

Continuous improvement is a systemic perspective that is critical to this entire model. You may be at the top of the ladder today, but how will you stay there? Making decisions at the top requires a different mindset from the one that got you there. Never stop growing, and never ignore the information and resources around you.

Who Can Use the Factors?

We're giving you the complete package to become a strategic leader from the ground up, but we also know there are many people in leadership positions already who need to strengthen their strategic capabilities. Once you're thinking and communicating like a strategic leader, it's time to apply your knowledge and skills throughout your organization. Being strategic is important if you want to earn the respect of other leaders, but that only gets you so far. You need to guide your team, get results, show what you've done, and continuously improve. Factors two through six will address the things strategic leaders do to run a successful, winning organization. If you're not yet in a role with systemic responsibilities, you will still learn a lot here. Begin by understanding what's currently happening with your organization's leadership. Are there higher ladder rungs that you can apply in your current role? Some of these ideas will support your personal development, such as establishing a vision and mission. Above all, look forward to the day when you can lead the strategic way. You don't need to wait for your business to ask you to be strategic or justify your budget; you can become strategic on your own and ensure your team is giving stakeholders the best possible return. It may seem like all the big decisions happen at the top, but truthfully every level has the opportunity to make strategic decisions. Big changes tend to happen when a lot of smaller changes come together—and the smarter and more strategic those smaller decisions are, the better chance the business has of winning.

Diana

As I mentioned early on, I learned a great deal from bosses who were not the strongest leaders, such as how it felt to be micromanaged, subject to commitments that were not kept, or working unsupported. Working under such leaders made me resolve to not treat people who reported to me like that. I also believe that if you offer positive and constructive suggestions to your bosses or leaders, many of them will be receptive and appreciative. They may even change these behaviors. One valuable lesson I learned as I had more people reporting to me was that it can be challenging to see all the results of your actions. Having employees who are willing to speak up is very helpful. Rembember, it's not usually the message we are delivering that gets people upset or defensive, but the way we say it and our timing. A good practice is to give positive feedback publicly and constructive feedback in private, in a caring way.

The model is flexible enough to be useful for any size of organization—you don't need a large governance board or seven-figure budget to align with your organization's strategy. If you're running your own small start-up, don't you want to make sure your decisions are having the best possible impact? How can you show your investors they will receive returns based on your actions? An important part of our model is knowing just how many options you have in your toolkit for making smarter decisions to help you win. Every factor in this book can be scaled up or down depending on your circumstances.

Diana

Although I grew up in a large, global organization, I now coach leaders in many smaller companies and find that the same principles apply. Over time, leaders tend to make the same mistakes over and over again, and you don't need a huge team or unlimited budget to learn how to stop making those mistakes and lead strategically.

Here's how Sam and Taylor choose to use our book:

Sam

I read most of the book on a long flight, through the lens of thinking about where my team is today and where we need to go. One thing I'm implementing right away is strategic think time, and my first agenda item for that time is to attack my weak areas in strategic leadership. I also asked some of my managers to read parts of the book, assigning different chapters depending on their areas of responsibility.

Taylor
I was working on a project with my counterpart in R&D, and he gave me a copy of the book. I flipped straight to the chapter on execution because I love getting stuff done. At some point, I'm going to go back to the chapter on governance, because that seems pretty intriguing.

Taylor will still benefit from her selective reading, but she is missing the whole point of our model, and of strategic leadership in general. The most well-planned execution isn't going to help you if you aren't aligned to your business—that is, if you're executing in the wrong jungle. Remember, you are building a ladder to the top of the jungle. Don't skip a rung if you aren't sure it's already firmly in place! Each chapter will include a short checklist to help you assess your current state for that factor.

A Quick and Dirty Framework for Strategic Leadership

The six factors provide a framework for strategic leadership, so we're giving them to you here again in a short graphic. Visit our companion website at www.bemorestrategicinbusiness.com to get a printable version of this graphic.

FACTOR 6: Make decisions to win

FACTOR 5: Execute your strategic plan

FACTOR 4: Build your strategic plan

FACTOR 3: Engage stakeholders

FACTOR 2: Establish the vision

FACTOR 1: Develop your foundational skills

Figure 2.1

Chapter 3

Factor 1—Develop Your Foundational Skills

Now that you are beginning to understand what a strategic leader looks like and how such leadership enables your organization to win, you are ready to make changes and develop your abilities. As you begin your work, you start with the role you're in today. You may not be running a department, leading a team, managing a budget, or advocating for your vision in the boardroom. Those are things you aspire to do, and so now is the time to prepare yourself to handle those kinds of responsibilities. What are you doing today that is holding you back from a strategic leadership role? Do you have a vision, even a blurry vision, for yourself as a leader? Do other leaders see you as strategic? Do you look and act the part?

What are you doing today that is holding you back from a strategic leadership role? Do you have a vision, even a blurry vision, for yourself as a leader? Do other leaders see you as strategic? Do you look and act the part?

The remainder of this chapter will help you assess where you are today and what you need to do in order to move up.

1. Expand Your Knowledge of the Inside and Outside of Your Organization

Know and talk about the big picture of your organization

You must be able to understand and articulate your company's vision, mission, and/or purpose, and then connect it back to everything you and your team are doing. In other words, you are always thinking about the system (your organization) as a whole. Strategic leaders speak regularly about the company's vision, and they ensure their people understand very clearly how the work of the team aligns with the vision. As a result, individual contributors and the overall team are more engaged and productive. Knowing the big picture also includes understanding how the company is performing in the market, as well as internal and external trends and how those impact the business. Not only must you grasp what's happening, but you must also be able to apply this knowledge in meaningful ways. In virtually every presentation former

McDonald's CEO Don Thompson made to audiences large and small, he consistently referenced the company's vision of "being our customers' favorite place and way to eat and drink." He also tied in the company's top three strategic priorities. As a result, the executives who thrived under his leadership knew that when they met with him to solicit support for any of their initiatives, they needed to be able to clearly articulate how the project aligned with the overall company vision and priorities.

> **Diana**
> I was proud that on the annual engagement survey, my team consistently achieved 100 percent agreement with the statement: "You understand how your work positively impacts the company's vision and strategic plan." When you lead a team, you use the company's vision as a screen to help ensure the team's work stays perfectly aligned. When team members have a clear understanding of how their work impacts the larger company, it is much easier for them (and for leaders) to identify the most important work. I started by understanding the larger system and cascaded it down to my team to build a "systems thinking" function.

By the same token, understand how you fit into the system and what value your function adds. The real value of your work is not the items on your performance review—it's how you contribute to overall business goals.

Be informed about your organization's inner workings

If you've spent the majority of your career siloed in a department (e.g., a learning department, marketing, IT, etc.), whether as an independent contributor or a virtual employee, you may not be deeply acquainted with the way your business is run. It's okay to admit you don't know the basic measures on your P&L; it's not okay to remain ignorant of these critical numbers. It's also not okay to guess at what you think the business is up to. Take the time to find out what's really happening and stay up to date! We're going to give you some ideas for how to get started, but understand that you are looking for information about your specific, unique organization. The way your organization talks about success may very well be different from the examples we use here. Network with your colleagues in finance to really get acquainted with the numbers and learn the language of the business.

Your company's P&L (profit and loss statement) is a good place to start. If you work for a publicly held company, this is easy to find online. If your company is privately held, you may need to do some digging to gain access (again, befriend the folks in finance). Here you should see things like revenue growth, operating expenses, and net income. As you get used to looking at financial statements, financial pain points should become clear, and you will also be able to see positive and negative trends over time. Likewise, your company's annual report is another treasure trove of information. Here you will learn what the board of directors and top management are focused on, and what numbers they use to determine the health of the organization. Again, for public companies, these reports are available online. If you're working for a nonprofit organization, you may look for materials prepared for donors and stakeholders. Grant applications can be another source. And while you're at it, peek through your competitor's annual report and compare it to yours. How is their vision and strategy different? Can you identify any gaps that you can leverage?

As you review these documents, you're learning about how your company makes money. This sounds like it should be a simple concept—our income source is the products or services we offer. But when you dive into the numbers, you realize it's more complex, particularly for very large organizations with many layers of operations.

Not only do you need to know how your company makes money, but you must also know how leadership accounts for profits and talks about successes and failures. As you learn about the key financial metrics, your colleagues in HR can fill in the picture with people metrics. Numbers like turnover, engagement, and staffing levels are closely linked to what you've seen on your company's P&L. The organization's people, or talent, are directly responsible for driving the financial metrics in that they create, deliver, and sell the company's products and/or services. You must understand how your department is linked to business measures, and from here it becomes much more straightforward to prioritize your own initiatives. You begin to see which business metrics you can realistically influence.

There are other business metrics you may come across. Customer metrics, such as satisfaction levels and retention, are critical because the business makes its income from its customers. These may look different depending on whether your organization sells to other businesses, consumers, or both. While you may not technically have a direct link to your external or internal customers, you do have an indirect link to them. Also, don't forget about compliance issues. If you operate in a highly regulated environment, such as food, banking, or pharmaceuticals, then you are likely very familiar with compliance needs. But every organization must comply with certain financial reporting rules, employment regulations, and environmental concerns. These areas can offer explanations for numbers you may even see on your company's P&L, as being non-compliant with various laws and regulations can be very costly for a business.

Learn what's happening around you and incorporate that knowledge into your everyday vocabulary

Strategic leaders know what's happening in the marketplace and how it will impact the organization. They constantly think about the near and far future. If you want to participate in conversations with top executives and other leaders, you need a strong command of relevant trends. There is so much information about companies that is easily accessible on the internet. We suggest you regularly read your company's website and other industry literature. Don't forget about the company's annual report. Be at least as educated about your company as the average consumer could be. Make the time to read important news about your company at least once a week, if not daily. Set up Google alerts for your company and leadership so you are always current and in the know. If you lack business acumen and skills, watch videos online or take a business course. This isn't a nice-to-do thing; it's critical if you want to stay relevant and build your big-picture thinking abilities. Talk to other people throughout the organization, particularly those who work in functions you don't interact with on a day-to-day basis. If possible, get the customer perspective on your business, too—visit a store where nobody knows you, or hire your company to perform its flagship service. What does it feel like to be on the other side? Oh, and don't keep the information to yourself. Share it with others to help educate the people around you and to shape future strategies and actions. You will appear knowledgeable, informed, engaged, and proactive.

Become well-versed in your professional field

What are others in your field or discipline doing to stay ahead of trends and conquer challenges? Networking with your industry peers will give you a perspective that's broader than the priorities on your plate today. They'll offer different perspectives, experiences, and information. If you're too internally focused, you may miss big opportunities to shift. Even if you work in a field that's highly proprietary, there are still opportunities to learn from what your competitors are doing. How do they interact in the market? What are their customers saying?

If you don't have a big existing network and aren't a regular on the conference scene, there are still lots of ways to dive in. LinkedIn is a low-pressure way to reach out to individuals and find smaller networking groups. Many regular publications, large and small, share who's winning and what's trending. There is so much information online about companies, and you must make the time to do your research. Become proactive; understand where your industry is going, what the top organizations are doing, and how you can improve on their ideas in your own organization.

A note of caution when it comes to benchmarking: as you look at other organizations, ensure that you understand all the factors that led to their successes. If you're going to apply what worked for your competitors, you need to ensure it's applicable to your company. Here's what we mean. In the mid-1990s, United Airlines created a new service, Shuttle by United, to try to go after Southwest Airlines' market share in California.

> The gate staff and flight attendants wore casual clothes. Passengers weren't served food. Seeking to emulate Southwest's legendary quick turnarounds and enhanced productivity, Shuttle by United increased the frequency of its flights and reduced the scheduled time planes would be on the ground. None of this, however, reproduced the essence of Southwest's advantage—the company's culture and management philosophy, and the priority placed on employees. Southwest wound up with an even higher market share in California after United had launched its new service.[9]

The United example shows where benchmarking was more like imitating. It was poorly done, and it ended up being to United's detriment. You aren't looking to put lipstick on a pig when you benchmark. You want to learn from others' successes, incorporate what may work in your case, and put your own spin of ingenuity on top.

2. Change Your Thinking

Focus on results and goals

Once you start to see the big picture of your organization and market, your mind will naturally turn to vision and strategy. Strategic leaders always have the vision at the forefront of everything they do. The vision is the fundamental reason why you do what you do—whether it's the big vision of your company as a whole, or your personal vision for your own life. Having a defined vision gives you a guidepost for making decisions about what to do and how to do it. Without a vision, you're running around like a crazy person from one thing to the next. All of the learning we talked about in the section above feeds into your understanding of the vision. You need the background knowledge in order to process what's happening and plan for the future in a way that encompasses the big picture. Chapter 5 will teach you how to craft a vision, mission, and strategy.

9 https://hbr.org/2006/01/evidence-based-management

Follow a personal vision to guide your priorities and ensure you have the energy to be strategic

Chances are, when you picked up this book, you had at least one professional ambition in mind that you hoped we would help you achieve. Once you have that personal vision in place, you need to assess the rest of your life. Do you have a support system in place that enables you to focus your energy where you need to? Are you taking on tasks that could be delegated elsewhere, freeing you up to spend time with the people you love and doing the things that make you happy? Set goals, and then structure your life in a way that will ensure you can achieve them. We all have the same twenty-four hours in a day, or 1,440 minutes, no matter who you are or what you do. It's up to you to choose to use each minute in the best, most strategic way.

When you have opportunities at work, make sure you're able to take advantage of them. What this means is different for everyone, but we've known many smart, hard-working leaders who've burned out because they think they have to do it all at work *and* at home. We also know leaders who were so bogged down and/or afraid they passed on great opportunities that they later regretted. So as you put your priorities in place and figure out what's truly important for you to do yourself, don't forget to build in the basics of taking care of yourself: eating well, exercising, relaxing/recovering, and sleeping.

> **Diana**
> Early in my career, I learned a valuable lesson that ultimately made me successful moving forward, across every aspect of my life. I was the classic example of the busy, exhausted, stressed-out executive trying to squeeze family into my overloaded life. I believed that people succeeded by giving 110 percent at work, and although I felt drained all the time, there was always more work to do. When my daughters were five and three years old, I experienced a harsh wake-up call in the form of an aggressive kidney infection. After being hospitalized to fight off the infection, I faced a long recovery process. It was during this time that I realized just how out of whack my priorities had been. Taking care of myself by eating well, getting

enough sleep, and exercising regularly had to come before everything else—being so critically ill had shown me that I couldn't expect to handle anything else in my life without my health. I share this story because it's my hope that I can keep other leaders from going through the same type of experience. When I eventually went back to work, I put in fewer hours, but they were much more productive because I wasn't so burned out. My relationships with my beloved family members improved because I was mentally present when I was with them.

Stacey

I was unexpectedly diagnosed with an aggressive form of cancer at the age of thirty-five, when my daughter was a baby. My doctors told me to go home and put my affairs in order; they said I likely had fewer than five years to live. I very quickly learned to prioritize who and what is important in my life: what did I want to do in five years that I would leave behind for my little girl? As it turned out, those doctors were wrong, but they gave me the gift of a very concrete sense of how I wanted to raise my daughter. I was always into fitness, but exercise became crucial for my survival. Today, everyone in my life knows that the first two hours of the day are mine to spend at the gym. This time is blocked on my calendar and is non-negotiable. When it's done, I'm set up—emotionally and physically—to be there for my clients and family for the rest of the day.

As you look at the big picture of your responsibilities, both at work and outside of work, you have to decide what is the most important. Ask yourself:

- Where do you want to show up and bring your A game?
- What gives you energy and makes you feel driven?
- What tasks aren't energizing to you?

- What can you realistically delegate or outsource?
- Are you saying yes to things that aren't in your best interest?
- Are you spending your time on the things that align with your top priorities?

Let those top priorities be your guideposts. No one else can define this for you—it's your opportunity to chart the path of your own success. It's a given that you'll get distracted at times, but with a clear plan and vision for your life, you'll be able to get back on track. If you're prone to saying yes to everything, it's also easier to say no when you can see what aligns to your own personal and professional goals. All of that said, life isn't black and white! There will be times when you need to work more, and there will also be times when your personal life needs you more. It's up to you to identify those times and integrate life's different aspects as you can.

Carve out and use regular time for strategic thinking

You can't be strategic if you're constantly mired in the weeds of everyday operations (i.e., on the jungle floor with the producers). While it's critical to stay in touch with your team, you also need to put capable managers in place so that you can maintain your focus on the big picture and envision the future. Strategic leaders schedule regular thinking time, away from distractions. Committing to regular thinking time and really doing it will make you more successful.

Step back. Sit down. Maybe even stare out the window and just think. Don't multitask. As a matter of fact, neuroscience research has recently discovered that humans don't really do tasks simultaneously; we switch tasks quickly.[10] Task switching involves a stop/start process, which is time-consuming; even in microseconds, that can add up quickly. It's more efficient to focus on one task even for a short while, and then switch to the new task. Only by focusing your thoughts can you continue to ensure a strong connection to your stakeholders and the core of your business or mission as the

---

10 http://www.apa.org/research/action/multitask.aspx

environment changes; ensure your team is achieving the desired results and having the necessary impact on the organization; and confidently determine adjustments that may be in order. Finding extra think time can feel impossible for busy executives with plates that are already too full. You have to make the time to think.

Anticipate the consequences of your decisions and make your thinking more transparent

Not only do strategic leaders try to understand long-term consequences before making decisions, but they model that behavior for their team members to help direct reports build their own decision-making capabilities.

Imagine Taylor has found a vendor to develop a program at 50 percent of the amount spent to develop a previous program of similar scale. Taylor is excited to show these cost savings to build consensus for deploying the new program. In the planning meeting with Taylor, Sam asks, "If we go that route, how would we maintain the program if and when we need to make updates or change the content?" Taylor hasn't considered the long-term implications of her proposed solution. She goes back to the vendor and learns that any maintenance or updates would need to be contracted through them since the program will be built in their proprietary software. She then needs to reconfigure her budget to account for future changes, and it turns out that the program will actually be more expensive over time than its predecessor. Sam knew to look at the total cost of ownership (including direct and indirect costs) for the program—not just the immediate investment, but the long-term costs that make up the true cost of the program. Sam's also being transparent in her reasoning. She could've simply shut Taylor down, knowing the new program would actually be more expensive. Instead, she encourages Taylor to think through the details and come to the same conclusion. This is strategic peer-to-peer coaching.

Strategic leaders help build their employees' skills through this kind of dialogue, too. You also stand to learn more about your people along the way. High performers and future leaders will welcome these developmental exchanges, whereas lower performers and those with little leadership potential may become defensive. Later in this book, we'll introduce the Impact Blueprint, which is a graphical tool that shows how you can think through the impact of your investments and link them to business outcomes. As you work through the process of creating your own blueprint, you'll uncover potential consequences of your decisions, which in turn will help you make smarter decisions.

3. Look and Act Strategic

We've never been big fans of the phrase, "fake it till you make it," but it does apply here to some extent. It doesn't mean to be fake—it means to consciously work hard on your new skill set until it becomes natural for you. Start acting like a strategic leader, even if you aren't one yet! An important part of succeeding as a leader is giving people the confidence to follow you. In fact, evolutionary psychologists argue that some forms of self-deception (faking it) show that there are social rewards (making it)[11]. When you think you are something that you may not be, you are less insecure and others perceive your confidence as competence. If you start to look and act strategic, you will be perceived as strategic while you're learning. As you get higher in your organization and have a greater scope of responsibilities, you can't possibly keep a grasp of every little detail. What you can do is ask the right questions and keep your people focused on the vision. You may not have the answers, but they know how to look for alignment with the vision and uncover unintended consequences.

Be accountable and foster a culture of accountability

Think about some of the best customer service experiences you've had. For most people, what comes to mind is a time when a company screwed something up and handled it well. Maybe your rental car wasn't available when you stepped off a delayed flight, and you were under a tight timeline to make it to an important meeting. You expected the clerk at the desk to roll his eyes and point you toward the cab line, but instead, he took ownership of the problem. He apologized (even though you know it wasn't his personal fault), and he fixed it by driving you to your meeting and coming back later with the car you'd reserved.

11 http://humancond.org/papers/evolution_and_psychology_of_self-deception

That rental clerk, there on the front lines of the organization, understands what it means to be accountable and strategic. He knows that he represents his employer, and that any good company wants to do everything in its power to deliver on its brand promise. His company is likely one that regularly shows its employees how valuable they are and empowers them to make decisions related to the strategy. You don't need to be the CEO to make strategic-level contributions!

The book *The Oz Principle* defines accountability as follows:

> An attitude of continually asking, "what else can I do to rise above my circumstances and achieve the results I desire?" It is the process of "seeing it, owning it, solving it, and doing it." It requires a level of ownership that includes making, keeping, and proactively answering for personal commitments. It is a perspective that embraces both current and future efforts rather than reactive and historical explanations.[12]

Being accountable and strategic go hand in hand. Both require a systems mindset that sees a problem and automatically thinks, how can I make this better? It's the exact opposite of the phrase you may have heard if you've spent much time in a dysfunctional workplace: "That's not my job." You may not own the problem, but if it's a problem in your organization, then it is in fact your problem. When you're a strategic leader and building a culture of accountability, it doesn't mean you run around doing everyone else's job—far from it! It means you're making sure that everyone on your team is doing his or her part to drive performance toward the relevant organizational goals. Your job is to remove barriers so your team can succeed. When something goes wrong, you own the problem and figure out how to fix it—whether that's actually fixing it yourself or bringing it to the attention of the person who can. We love *The Oz Principle's* four steps for accountability:

> The first step—See It—involves recognizing and acknowledging the full reality of a situation. [...] The

12 *The Oz Principle* Roger Connors, Tom Smith, and Craig Hickman. p65. 2009

second step—Own It—means accepting responsibility for the experience and realities you create for yourself and others. With this step, you pave the road to action. The third step—Solve It—entails changing reality by finding and implementing solutions to problems that you may not have thought of before…. And the fourth, the "Do It" step, entails mustering the commitment and courage to follow through with the solutions you have identified, even if those solutions involve a lot of risk.[13]

Reserve the right to get smarter as you go along. Ask yourself, Have I been accountable as far as delivering business results? How would I rate myself?

As the strategic leader of an accountable team, you understand the goals, identify what needs to be done, and organize the work in a way that makes sense. You assign the best people to accomplish each task, and then you measure progress to ensure you're making progress toward the goals. You're accountable for the actions that bring the vision to life. Your team knows why they're doing what they're doing, and they also have a strong grasp of who's doing what.

Accountable leaders are results-focused, and those results are aligned to the right goals. Coming back to the jungle analogy, the managers who said, "Shut up! We're making progress!" are the epitome of lack of accountability. What they're doing is pointless, but they want credit for doing something! An accountable leader also seeks personal feedback to ensure she continues to improve as a leader. Reserve the right to get smarter as you go along. Ask yourself, *Have I been accountable as far as delivering business results? How would I rate myself?* If you need to reverse direction on a poor decision, own your mistake and make the necessary change. Watch how others in your organization handle mistakes. Do they hold themselves accountable? How do they do that? What do they say?

13 Ibid.

Honestly assess your personal appearance

Take a hard look at the leadership culture in your company. Can you see yourself fitting in with these folks? There's such a wide variety of acceptable dress standards today across companies and industries. The important thing is to understand the level of your organization and adapt to it. If your executive team members wear suits every day, you can't expect to start attending board meetings wearing a polo and khakis. But if you're working in a more casual culture, a suit may be the garment that makes you look out of place. The same goes for things like your hairstyle, facial hair, fingernails, and other areas of personal grooming. No, you don't have to look exactly like your CEO. But you also shouldn't stick out like a sore thumb. Your appearance should support your aspirations to leadership, not create a barrier that others have to overcome in order to see you as strategic. Same goes for personal behaviors, such as your body language, mannerisms, and way of speaking. You may have habits that work against you and not even be aware of them. Ask a few trusted colleagues for feedback.

> **Diana**
> I've been in a number of meetings with executive leaders where we were discussing promotions and an executive didn't think a certain leader was ready to move up because that individual wasn't coming across as strategic. That could be related to the individual's appearance, communication, persona, or something else giving the sense that others will not follow this person. I'd say, "When is the last time you worked with him?" and the executive would say, "Well, it's been about two years." It wasn't always easy to make a case for somebody who I knew deserved a promotion, but others didn't have the same perception. I would share the feedback with the individual, but other leaders don't always do that. Ultimately, it's up to you to find out what could be holding you back and make the necessary changes.

If you're already perceived as a tactical leader, you have your work cut out for you, but your image isn't set in stone! Consider your image with each individual leader as a snapshot in time. They are going to continue to believe the impression you've given them in the past, and it's up to you to update that snapshot. You are the owner of other people's impressions of you.

> **Stacey**
> Once I see a leader as strategic, I find it easier to buy into what he is saying because I know he's already thought it through and connected it to the bigger picture. Conversely, if I don't have the impression that the leader is strategic, I automatically question everything. If you can teach others to perceive you as strategic, it becomes that much easier to get your job done!

Your physical appearance, behavior, body language, and mannerisms are typically easy to change if they are serving as barriers to you coming across as strategic. This isn't about changing who you are. It's about self-awareness and showing that you're going to fit in, that people will follow you, and that you fit into the image that leadership wants. You can make the changes or choose not to—but if you choose not to, consider what you're giving up. You're not going to get the chance to lead if leaders don't feel comfortable with you. Dress with what you're comfortable with and think about the message you're giving. Are others comfortable with the way you're dressing? Is your appearance creating unnecessary barriers that you may not have considered?

Evolve your communication style

Your communication style is the most critical way you show others that you are strategic, and it's also how you're able to get things done. It's so important we've devoted an entire chapter to it, so keep reading to learn how strategic leaders communicate

Make your calendar work for you

Evaluate the way you schedule everything in your day. Are you running from meeting to meeting without a moment to catch your breath? Are you consistently late, or is it hard to engage at the beginning of a discussion because you're still mentally stuck in the conversation from your last call? If so, you need to learn to be more judicious with your schedule. When you accept an invitation to a meeting, make sure you are also including time to be prepared for the discussion, as well as to be both mentally and physically present. Start evolving your calendar so you aren't rushing around. When you're doing that, you look like a tactical, overworked person, which doesn't bode well when leadership is considering who should receive additional responsibilities. You also can't bring your best self into meetings when you can't catch your breath in between. Learn how to manage your time in a way that honors your need to digest what you've heard and prepare for the next event.

Stephen Covey, in his book *The 7 Habits of Highly Effective People*, provides a matrix for managing your time that is a useful tool if you're struggling with an overly full calendar. To use the matrix, you classify your activities in the following way:[14]

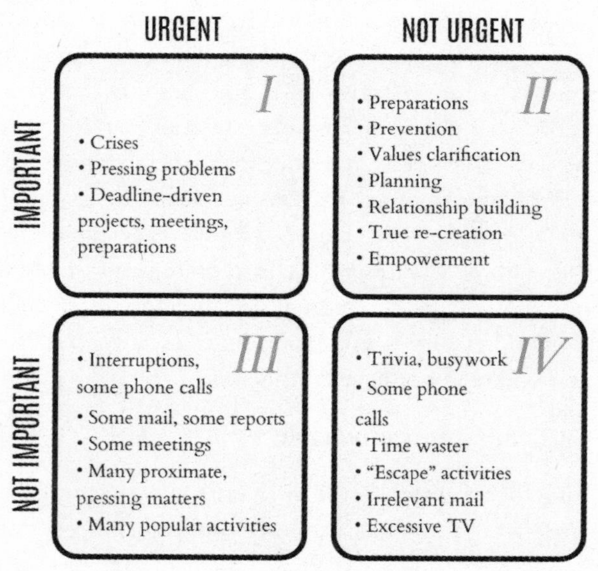

Figure 3.1

The second quadrant, important but not urgent, is where strategic leaders should spend most of their time. If you're always wrapped up in the important and urgent activities, you lose sight of the big picture (wrong jungle!) and also never get to the important,

14 *Covey Leadership Center* workbook. P 85. 1996.

non-urgent items. Depending on your current position, you probably can't make over your calendar overnight. You can, however, start thinking about what you want it to look like and create screens for yourself to use when deciding whether to accept meeting invitations.

As you adjust your time management, people will learn how to treat your calendar. By leaving a minimum of 15 minutes between meetings, you give yourself white space to deal with the things that inevitably pop up: urgent emails, phone calls, or a quick catch-up with someone who needs a decision from you. As things come up, strategic leaders are approachable and reachable; you shouldn't allow anyone to suck up all your time, but you do need to be able to react in a timely manner. Keep flexibility in your day.

Where Do You Begin?

You can't change your life overnight, but you can start a journey to being energized, fueled, and set up to think, look, and act more strategic. Choose two to three things to get you started. Here are some ideas:

- What is your vision for your life, both personally and professionally? Do you have concrete, measurable goals? It's ok if your vision is a little blurry, but you need some direction.
- What does your calendar look like? Put fifteen minutes between your appointments and show up prepared.
- Where are you spending your time? Are you focused on the not important and not urgent tasks, or are you dedicated to the priorities you established for yourself? Are there things you should be removing or adding on?
- Do you know your weaknesses? How can you turn these into strengths?
- What does your company stand for? If you can't clearly answer that, build in time to start learning.
- What are the gaps in your knowledge that can be closed by networking with a purpose? What do you need to

know and learn, and who can help you accomplish that? If you don't have a budget for traveling and conferences (or even if you do!), get active on LinkedIn.

- What do the successful officers and leaders in your company look like? Does your energy, attitude, and appearance reflect theirs?
- Keep reading! There's a lot more to come.

Many professionals employ an outcome visualization technique attributed to Aristotle.[15] Professional athletes, Olympians, musicians, surgeons, trial attorneys, and many others visualize themselves in the environment performing the required task. If you can self-visualize, then you can use that mental image to think through the process and the end result. Visualize yourself in the boardroom if that's where you aspire to be. How do you appear? How do you fit in? How do you behave? How do you engage your peers? What do you contribute?

Enlist a Personal Development Board to Help You

Are you familiar with the concept of a governance board? If not, don't worry—it'll be addressed in a later chapter. We apply a model similar to a governance board to help you in your own strategic leadership journey. We believe that everyone should have a personal board, made up of the people around you who have additional knowledge and experience that you can learn from. Your personal board helps you to develop as a strategic leader by giving you honest feedback and occasionally advocating for you where needed. You're probably familiar with the concept of a mentor, or maybe you even have one. Your personal board is broader than a mentor in that you get input from multiple people in carefully chosen positions. A personal board is like your career support group. By combining the perspectives of multiple leaders, you weed out individual biases. Your personal board members see you interact across the organization, and they're willing to help coach you to become more strategic and successful. If you are a consultant or an independent contributor, your personal board may be former

15 https://www.huffingtonpost.com/frank-niles-phd/visualization-goals_b_878424.html

clients, current or former managers, current or former colleagues, and/or industry experts. You already have the ability to be great. Now you need people with outside perspectives on what you need to do differently to get there, and perhaps to help provide the right resources too.

How do you know whom to invite to your personal board?

As you read the description of the personal board, did anyone pop into your mind? Do you interact with a leader who is inspiring, smart, and makes you want to do better? It's our hope that you have a few people like this in your organization, and we recommend selecting about three of them. If you're having trouble coming up with names, ask yourself who you know who fits one or more of the following:

- Has a reputation for being strategic rather than tactical, and understands the big picture of what the company is trying to achieve
- Demonstrates the leadership capabilities in chapters 1 and 2, particularly those you lack
- Is good at thinking through decisions and evaluating options transparently, so you can learn from his thinking
- Is well-respected in the organization
- Will stretch your thinking
- Will be honest with you, sharing what she sees you do well and where you have opportunities to get better
- Sits in a position where he has the knowledge and skills that would supplement what you already bring to the table

The biggest mistake you can make when building your personal board is selecting your fan club, or people who are just like you.

The biggest mistake you can make when building your personal board is selecting your fan club, or people who are just like you.

They tend to create an echo chamber, and they won't offer the sometimes-difficult opportunities you need to learn and grow. If at all possible, get feedback from your own leader. Let her know what you're trying to do and share the names you have in mind. If you have a supportive boss who takes the time to help you develop, you may ask her to be on your board. In many cases, this can be a sensitive situation if a manager feels threatened by your desire to grow. Perhaps you appear to be going after her job! You need to carefully read the situation and determine if your boss is a good person to ask for feedback. Be careful not to create a situation or relationship that can be used against you in the future. In general, you want to make sure anybody you share your aspirations with is going to be supportive. Sharing with someone who is competing against you isn't likely to help. If you can't find enough people to serve on your board, consider supplementing with an outside coach.

Now that you have your list, resist the urge to be intimidated. Your instinct may be that a certain leader is too busy or doesn't have the time to devote to you. Truthfully, most people are flattered to be asked for help, and if they're not willing or able to give it, they'll tell you just like a strategic leader does. Don't take it personally if someone says no. Chances are that person is being strategic with his time and is trying to stay true to his own set of personal priorities. When you're ready to ask, here is a sample email template that you can adapt to suit your situation:

> **Subject: Can you help me improve?**
>
> Hello (Stakeholder's name),
>
> I'm reaching out to see if you would be willing to help me improve as a strategic leader by serving as a personal stakeholder for me.
>
> I recently read the book *Be More Strategic in Business* and am working on strengthening my leadership competencies. Part of the book recommends identifying stakeholders to create my own personal version of a governance board. What I liked about the approach is that it is focused on identifying a few key leadership behaviors to improve, using a process involving stakeholders and with accountability for improvement.

Would you agree to be my stakeholder as I work on the following:

- Give two or three items you want your personal board to help you with

I will also ask for your willingness to be open and honest with me. If you see barriers to me becoming a strategic leader, I want to know about them so I can work to overcome them.

If you can help me, please reply to this email, and I will be in touch with you to describe the next steps.

Thank you,
Your name

What do you do with a personal board?

When you ask busy people to give up their time to help you, you'd better be clear about what you want from them right from the start. Put your strategic communication style into practice—what is your vision, what are your goals, and what can each board member help you accomplish? It's up to you whether you want to meet with your board members individually or as a group; we've found individual meetings to be easier and more effective, but you may find otherwise. The earlier chapters of this book have given you a lot of material for self-assessment. Hone in on the areas for improvement you've identified, but also be open to the observations and feedback of your personal board members. You may think your communication, physical appearance, or sense of accountability is fine, but do others see you the same way you do? Your personal board should complement the things you're trying to do and should fit into the time you have available for self-development. Make sure you share your personal vision so they understand where you're going, as well as your behavioral strengths, opportunities, and personal development plan.

Quick and Dirty Takeaways from This Chapter

Regardless of where you're starting, make the commitment to win. We've given you a lot of tactics in this chapter that you can use to build out your plan to get there. Here are a few things to remember.

- **Create your own development plan.** Review the strategic leadership competencies and figure out where you're acting like Sam and where you're more Taylor. Come up with a plan for improving on the areas where you need to be less tactical and more strategic.
- **Are you in the right jungle?** A strategic leader keeps an eye above the tree line in order to maintain focus on what's important.
- **You probably have a lot to learn.** Expand your knowledge about your organization, the market, your specific field, and business acumen.
- **Create a vision for your life and use it to align your priorities.** Don't let yourself become the exhausted and stressed leader. Create a life that supports what you aspire to do and focus your energy on the things that are important to you.
- **Rethink your calendar.** You need white space to think strategically, to prepare for appointments, and to respond to issues that pop up and require your attention.
- **Look and act the part.** Make an honest assessment of your personal appearance and persona or ask a trusted advisor to give you feedback. Are you unintentionally holding yourself back from being seen as strategic?
- **Every leader should have a personal development board.** These are the people who help you to stretch and grow, and they also give you an accurate assessment of how you're perceived as a leader.

Chapter 4

Communicate

Thinking strategically is only half the battle. Once you are thinking and acting strategically, you need to learn to communicate in a way that serves your cause. You can be doing all the right things, developing your strategic leadership capabilities, making smart decisions, and getting better results. But it's all for naught if you can't tell your story in a way that captures your listener's attention and gets your desired result. When you're a strategic leader, you're always thinking through your intentions as they relate to where the organization is going. Your communication must reflect that. At every point of contact with employees, customers, stakeholders, and other leaders, strategic leaders consider two key things:

- *Why* am I communicating?
- *How* will I convey my message in order to get my desired result?

By thinking through these two questions before communicating, you can build a professional practice of communicating strategically, which will in turn show other leaders that you *are* strategic. Strategic leaders communicate with intention in every interaction—whether they are leading a team meeting, presenting to stakeholders, pitching to investors, or happen to take a thirty-second elevator ride with the CEO. Every conversation is an opportunity to advance your vision. Remember the McDonald's CEO we mentioned in chapter two? His executives knew that they needed to always reference his vision when they met with him. Everything they did had to align with being the McDonald's customer's favorite place and way to eat and drink. But it wasn't enough for the executive to know the alignment was there—she needed to communicate that alignment to the CEO. This is a key difference in strategic leaders that must come across when you communicate: you don't throw out a great idea and expect others to connect the dots. You pitch your idea in the context of the vision.

Diana

One of my coaching clients came to me with an incredibly strong ability to think strategically. I quickly realized his problem was that he couldn't show this ability to his leadership. Although he had smart and relevant things to say, his way of saying them was all over the place. As he worked on communicating with intention, other leaders began to see him as strategic. The content of his message was essentially the same, but the way he presented it made all the difference.

In the last chapter, we talked about how your appearance and body language can prevent others from seeing you as strategic. Communication is the other piece of that. You need to learn how to connect with your audience in a way that engages them, and ultimately gets them to support your vision. Start paying close attention to the way other leaders around you communicate. You'll notice the differences between strategic communicators and those who are more tactical. You become more effective by honoring where your audience is and what they want. From there, you can learn to give information in a way that highlights what's important for your audience to hear from you. This type of thinking may require effort at first, but it will eventually become natural for you if you keep practicing it.

Before we teach you how to communicate like a strategic leader, we're going to let Taylor and Sam give an example to illustrate the differences. In this example, Sam and Taylor are marketing directors in a small start-up that has been generating new customers using Facebook ads. They've been working closely with the CEO, June, to get the content for these ads just right, and June has decided it's time for her to be less hands on with the day-to-day mechanics of running these ads. A few weeks later, June is heading out of the country, trusting her team to run the business while she's gone. Taylor calls June on the day of her departure:

> June: Hi Taylor, I have five minutes before my flight boards. What's up?
>
> Taylor: Ok, well, I just wanted to quickly inform you that the click-through rates on our ads have dropped in the past couple weeks. We went from over 2 percent click-throughs

down to only 0.5 percent. So, um, basically we're spending the same amount of money as we did last month, but there are fewer clicks.

June: Hmm. Has that affected the number of leads coming in?

Taylor: Oh, good question. Let me look...

June: Okay, let me know about that when—

Taylor: Oh wow! Actually, we've gotten the same number of leads. Our conversions are up since we made that new landing page.

June: Okay, good. So at least we are keeping the sales team busy.

Taylor: Yup! So I guess no problem here then.

Now let's replay the same situation, with Sam in the role of marketing director.

June: Hi Sam, I have five minutes before my flight boards. What's up?

Sam: Hey, we can chat more about this when you're back, but I wanted to give you a heads-up that we're going to start tweaking the ads to make sure we maintain the same level of inbound leads.

June: Oh man, but I love those ads, and we put so much time into them!

Sam: Yeah, me too. But fewer people are clicking, and I think that changing up the images will help recapture the attention of people who have already seen them a bunch of times. We can always save the old ads and run them again at another time.

June: Gotcha. Okay, I'm excited to see what you come up with.

Let's break these interactions down and look at why the outcomes are so different. First, both marketing directors have caught June at a bad time. Taylor immediately peppers June with numbers and waits for her to figure out the significance of those figures. Sam presents the solution and waits for June to ask why she has made this decision. When June does ask, Sam doesn't give actual figures, but presents the *significance* of the metrics she's monitoring—Sam starts with the reason *why* she's making the call. She indicates that she can share details when June has more time. Taylor is looking at her dashboard of data while she's on the phone—had she looked at the number of leads, she might not have even needed to pick up the phone. However, it's a good thing she did, because now June can see that Taylor isn't thinking about the long-term performance of the ads. Sure, the sales team is busy today, but with fewer ad clicks, will that pace of inbound leads keep up? But again, Taylor has picked a bad time to call June and bring this up. Sam, on the other hand, hears (and probably anticipated, having collaborated with her during the development process) June's emotional attachment to the ads, and responds to that. Even though she's telling June that she wants to set a different direction from the one June has established, Sam's doing it in a way that addresses June's objections.

Now consider the overall tone of the conversations. Both are quick and relatively casual, but Sam's message is pulled together. Taylor hasn't done her due diligence of looking at all the data (in this case, inbound leads) before calling June. Instead, she's raised what she thinks is a red flag without coming up with a potential solution. She's thinking through that solution right there on the phone with her boss. It's not that this is necessarily a bad thing to do—it's how many people learn to be strategic. Taylor, however, is in a role that should put her past that point. She shouldn't be asking for her boss' recommendation until she has laid out her approach to the problem and taken accountability for the solution. Sam, meanwhile, understands that her boss' time is valuable, and she also know it's not a good time to get into a deep conversation with June. She's taken ownership of the situation and is looking to get a quick blessing from June before moving forward. She also shows that she's in control of the situation—she monitored her success metrics, identified an issue, and has a solution ready to try.

Six Steps to Clear and Effective Communication

Communicating as a strategic leader is all about determining what information is important to share with your audience, and then sharing the information in a way that's enticing, that invites your audience to engage and ask questions, and that they can easily understand. You make your communication count by thinking about it first. It gets easier with practice! Here are five steps to help you focus.

You make your communication count by thinking about it first.

1. **Know yourself.** As you work on your ability to communicate like a strategic leader, it's important to be aware of your own strengths and areas for improvement. If you're an introvert, you may tend toward thinking things through before speaking up, which means you run the risk of not jumping in soon enough. If you're an extrovert, you probably like to think out loud and tend to say too much. By knowing your own habits, you can work on determining the right time to join a discussion, as well as how to organize what you have to say. You can use a personality assessment or strength finder to help you identify your own strengths and gaps, as well as those of your team members. By understanding yourself, you can use your preferred style, and then develop your weaker areas and/or hire to compensate for your gaps.

   Stacey
   I know my style, my strengths, and my blind spots. For instance, I have learned that I am a better leader when I have someone with the strength of empathy on my team to compensate for my overly analytical nature. I have a strong tendency to be goal-oriented and doggedly focused on outcomes, data, or processes at the expense of being tuned into the emotions of others—that Andersen performance review I recounted in the introduction

wasn't so far off base! Now that I am aware of my style and strengths, I know I need to surround myself with those who are better able to sense emotions. I try to use those people as my barometer to communicate more effectively. This doesn't mean I'm not empathetic; I'm actually a very empathetic person, but only when I'm not focused like a dog on a bone.

Diana

Throughout the years, my strengths have stayed pretty consistent: I'm strategic, a strong communicator, and an enthusiastic innovator. I have the ability to connect, motivate, and lead people. As an avid learner, I have continued to work on my areas of opportunity, such as slowing down, focusing on the details, and listening. My natural style is to want to move things forward and achieve results. I have learned to surround myself with people who are more analytical and good with details and who ensure things have been thought through. They help me to be a better leader and make better decisions.

If reading the room is hard for you, tap someone on your team who is good at it. He or she can give you subtle signals while you're speaking to help you identify when you're losing your audience. Remember, if a leader asks you what time it is, you don't need to tell her how to build a clock! Give a straightforward answer and let her ask for specifics.

2. **Know your audience.** Focus on the person or people with whom you're communicating. Who is your audience, and where are they coming from in the context of whatever topic you're discussing? Think about how you communicate in your personal life. If someone asks how your weekend was, your answer is going to vary based on whether the asker is your

mother, your coworker, your close friend, or your doctor. You might convey the same information to all four audiences, but even if you do, the way you present the story will vary widely. In business, you need to know what your audience cares about with respect to the topic at hand. What does he or she hope to get out of the conversation? Which details will be significant to whom? Why should he or she care about this topic?

In your own organization, it's relatively straightforward to know your colleagues and leaders. If you're a new employee or don't know someone, you can network and ask around. Try to be proactive, even if it's not your style. But what if you're meeting with customers, pitching investors, or speaking with the press? If you're going to be communicating with strangers, it's even more important to do your research. Find their online bios, look at what they've published, and see if you have any acquaintances in common. Be aware of what's going on with the organizations they represent, too. When possible, consider people's preferences: do they prefer lots of details? Do they prefer visual charts, tables of data, or narrative stories? Do they tend toward more formal or informal communication? Do what you can to determine these types of specifics.

Stacey

When I'm consulting with an organization for the first time, I try to learn as much as I can about the business, goals, and actors. I conduct an informal and formal needs analysis. Informally, I try to learn as much as I can about the actors, stakeholders, and organization. I will research and connect with as many as I can on LinkedIn. By connecting on LinkedIn, they can learn about me too so they know what my firm and I bring to the table. Of course, I have already thoroughly reviewed their website, annual reports, online publications, and anything else I can find to give me an idea of the current state of the business, their goals, and any strategic gaps my firm could fill. I will speak with my primary contact to brief me on the corporate culture, as well as each person's role, communication style, hot buttons, and general expectations. I also try to understand any group dynamics or politics that may affect my projects. I speak with other connections I have who may be familiar with the person, company, or industry. Formally, I ask for examples of successful and unsuccessful projects and why they succeeded or failed. For each project, I determine their current state and desired state and propose solutions to close the gaps that I know will work for their unique situation.

3. **Communicate with intention.** When you go into an interaction, have a clear objective: what end results are you trying to achieve? Sometimes this is obvious: I want to sell my services or gain approval for my budget. But even casual conversations can be intentional. If you find yourself in the elevator with your CEO, take advantage of that uninterrupted time! Instead of talking about how busy you are (which makes you look unfocused and tactical), mention great things that are happening or results you're excited about. Discussing results shows that you are focused on the right things and taking time to make sure you are in the right jungle. Show how you're aligned with the direction he's set for the company. You don't need to whip out a slide deck. Intentional communication is the difference between, "We're so busy, I was up until 2 a.m. last night finishing my report for the shareholders meeting," and, "Remember that pilot you approved last month? Customers are loving it, and we're really excited to be planning out phase two."

Discussing results shows that you are focused on the right things and taking time to make sure you are in the right jungle.

Here are a few questions to ask yourself to help screen your communication for intention:

- Does my message align with the vision of the company and my function?
- Will having this conversation enable me to act in a way that supports where we need to go?
- Is it critical that this information be shared at this time?
- Am I going to share the information in a way that is succinct and understandable?

If the answer to any of these questions is no, pause your thinking. Go back to your *why* for communicating and assess what needs to change so you can say yes to the four questions above. Maybe you'll realize you don't need to communicate at all, or it isn't the right time.

Diana

Another of my coaching clients was preparing to be the top learning leader in her company. She had a lot of great ideas and energy, and she was very passionate about her company. Though she was highly respected by her colleagues, the top leaders were concerned that her thinking wasn't at the level to take over the role of leading the learning department. We discovered that she did in fact have the ability to think big picture, connect the dots, think through the consequences, and determine the best route to move forward. Like so many others, her weakness was that she didn't communicate as clearly and concisely as she needed to show other leaders her true abilities. This is especially critical to do when you're in the presence of top leaders who have less exposure to the day-to-day you. They tend to make decisions about your abilities based on quick snapshots of time. My client was an extrovert and prone to thinking out loud, which made her come across as unfocused, overwhelmed, and at times confused. Through coaching, she learned to consciously slow herself down and think through what she wants to say before speaking. We worked on techniques to help her take a few seconds to think with intent before speaking, such as:

- Pausing with a purpose to reflect on what she wants

to say before she jumps in

- Not always being the first person to respond
- Asking others what they think before giving her opinion

I was thrilled to hear that she received a promotion because of the progress she has made on her ability to communicate and truly come across as a strategic leader.

Don't fall into the trap of over planning or avoiding interactions because you aren't fully prepared. By following the model in this book, you will ensure you're focused on the right things, which will give you the confidence to be calm and communicate as a strategic leader. Communication is an aspect of your development that will become stronger as you work on everything else. Here are a few ideas to have at the ready for casual interactions that will show you are a strategic thinker:

- Talk about something your team is doing that you're excited about and show how it supports what the broader organization is doing
- Read recent speeches or articles written by leadership and mention something you've seen that aligns with where the leader is going
- Mention a customer you've interacted with who is excited about a new product or service because it aligned with his or her expectations
- Discuss a shift in the industry you have learned about
- Present potential business or industry disrupters
- Share ideas you have that align to the corporate strategy, goals and vision even if it isn't related to your department or function

4. **Give the headlines.** As you work on communicating with intention, you quickly figure out what you want to get across. Now you need to think about how to get it across in the

most effective way. Begin by giving the WIIFM—what's in it for me—or in this case, for your audience. Now that you have really thought about your audience and know your end result, it's time to think through the best way to get there. If you were a reporter coming up with a headline for your story, what would sell the most papers? Give the important finding first and let them ask how you got there. Remember, you want to bring your audience along with you, so remember to engage them by giving them a little space to react to your feedback. Sometimes an engaging question is a good headline, especially if it addresses a current gap in organizational results. For example, "Would you be interested in a plan that would reduce our spending by 10 percent?" This is the same type of thinking you use when drafting presentation titles and email subject lines.

> **Stacey**
> To be honest, it took me a while to adapt to this communication style because it didn't come naturally to me. As a researcher and evaluator, I was trained to start with your hypotheses, and then collect and analyze your data to support or reject the hypotheses. Then present your findings. With input from performance reviews, peers, employers, mentors, and customers, and from working with sales professionals, I have learned the value of headlining. I used to think I should present in a format that builds up to the big reveal, but my presentations are always better received when I start with the "aha" and then tell them how I got there, if they want to know. Now, I often think that if my presentation or communication were a YouTube video, the key message is the thumbnail that helps viewers decide if they want to engage. Sometimes I'll even start with a little clickbait to get their attention.

5. **Put the person before the message.** Listen to your audience, acknowledge you've heard what they are saying, and let

them know you'll do something about it. The stronger the relationship you have with somebody, the more forgiving they're likely to be when you make mistakes or have to deliver bad news. If you can build a relationship with people before you need to communicate strategically with them, it will be easier for you to feel comfortable, as well as for them to understand where you're coming from. If you haven't been able to do that, go around the room and acknowledge each person. Arrive a few minutes early, and be sure that you know and use their names. Build a quick rapport wherever possible; by taking the time to look up people you don't know, you can offer small talk on a mutually interesting topic.

6. **Listen with the intent to hear.** One of the most critical keys to communicating effectively in any relationship is listening to hear. Strategic leaders do not just listen and say, "Yeah, yeah, I got it," or "No questions from me." They listen to what is being said and paraphrase what they've heard, asking questions until they sense mutual understanding. They don't start jumping to solutions. As others communicate with you, listen for potential obstacles and unexploited risks, as well as indications that people don't understand the goal or purpose of what they're doing. Listen for potential opportunities you hadn't thought of, too. Intent listening will help you determine if you are on the same page or whether there are flaws that need to be corrected. Strategic leaders have the ability to ask questions that help others to envision the future, assess risk and reward, and anticipate trends.

Stacey

My team and I frequently work remotely and present complex analytical findings in virtual settings. It's critical that our clients hear what we tell them so they can align our findings to their goals and strategy. It's also critical that we hear both what our client is and isn't saying. Since we can't read body language clearly in virtual settings, we are dependent on listening to tone and employing strong questioning techniques using frequent touch points. Most of the time we know that the people on the other end may be simultaneously working on something else and not listening to us, especially when the topic can be rather heady. We've learned that we can't present something complex and just ask, "Does that make sense? Are there any questions?" If we do that, we get back a lot of, "No questions now." To decide if we need to continue the discussion, we have to ask direct questions to specific people about what we presented to gauge their level of engagement. We will ask questions like:

- How do you think this finding can help achieve your goals?
- Which of these insights will you share with others?
- How can you apply this immediately, and what's the next step you will take?
- What was the most valuable insight we just discussed?

This line of questioning keeps them engaged in the conversation, tells us if we are being heard, and identifies needs for further clarification. Then, we will paraphrase what we heard them say to tighten up everyone's perspectives.

7. **Tune in to feedback and body language.** Once you share the headline and get into your presentation or discussion, look at the body language and facial expressions of the people you're speaking to. Are they glazing over or looking distracted? That indicates that you're giving too much detail and need to let them ask some probing questions, or that you didn't lead with the right information. If you talk too much, you don't give them a chance to engage with you or even react to what you're saying.

If you know who your audience is and that the information you're sharing is right for them, you can give headlines in a way that engages them and cover your topic succinctly and logically. Be interactive. Don't give too much information at one time. Make sure they've grasped what you've said byreading their body language and asking questions. These principles apply whether it's a quick, one-on-one conversation or a big, formal presentation. You always want to come across in a positive, can-do manner. By communicating in this way, you will be able to show your strategic leadership abilities.

But what if you're not in the same room, or even the same building? Virtual meetings present a whole other layer of challenges when it comes to reading the reactions of the people you're speaking with, particularly if there's no video feed.

Stacey

I consulted with a scientific organization to evaluate the effectiveness of a comprehensive industry training program and to design a program evaluation for the instructors to use in their classes. Once my work was done, I prepared a presentation of my recommendations and evaluation model to share with the stakeholders, some of whom were the instructors who were responsible for delivering the training. As it worked out, I presented to these instructors from out of state, which meant that they were all sitting in a conference room together with me on speakerphone and them on mute. During the call, there was dead silence on the other end of the phone, even when I probed for questions and asked for additional insights. At the end of my presentation, the instructors tersely thanked me and hung up with no willingness to discuss the evaluation findings or desire to establish an action plan. While my recommendations were in alignment with their needs, the leader who had hired my firm had failed to consider (or wasn't aware of) the cultural factors of my audience's expectations. These were highly skilled scientists who didn't appreciate having their program evaluated by a third party. They felt like it reflected poorly on their credibility. Also, they were not accustomed to working with consultants and

> were used being the only experts in the room. In the end, there was a significant political distraction, which included the organization's president. In hindsight, if my client had been better in tune with his internal customer stakeholders (the instructors), and if I had understood the organizational culture and networked more with the instructors, this could've been a different story. Needless to say, it was a short-lived engagement although an enormous learning opportunity.

When you have to present virtually, practice with somebody who knows the audience and play out possible political scenarios given the specific stakeholders involved. Use the headlines approach and find ways to get your audience to ask you for more details, which simultaneously keeps them engaged and allows you to virtually read the room. Don't feel restrained by your pre-planned communication structure or a tool you've used to prepare. It should feel natural.

When you're getting started, it's essential to practice! Take a video of yourself speaking so you can see how you come across. Do you look and sound the way you need and want to? Do you sound like Taylor or Sam? Get feedback from trusted advisors and people who witness your interactions. Do they think your communications convey that you've thought through the consequences of what you say? Do they see you connecting to the bigger picture, the strategic vision? You can also test out new communication techniques in a lower stakes situation, such as a team meeting—not only will you gain confidence, but you can see if others respond to you differently.

Navigating the Politics of Your Business

Another way to be an effective communicator is to understand how politics work in your company. Here's the straight, honest truth: politics is the way things get done in organizations. The more information you have, and the more champions who are on your side, the more successful and smooth your journey will be. If you simply don't care about politics, you will encounter barriers at every turn, and your job will be much more difficult as a result. You can use informal networks to help you accomplish what you want to accomplish, or you can resist those networks and let them work against you. You don't have to like it, but you do have to play by the rules (at least until you're in a position to change the political climate). Sometimes the way we do things in companies can look silly on its face, but when you dig into the politics of the situation, you learn that there is a lot more involved than a simple decision to change. That doesn't mean you can't make changes—it means you need to untangle what's behind the status quo first.

Here's the straight, honest truth: politics is the way things get done in organizations.

Diana

I began my McDonald's career at the age of sixteen, working in the restaurant after school. I worked my way up through the ranks over the years, building my career as I learned about almost every facet of the business. When I became a leader within the learning department, I learned about company politics as one of the very few female leaders at the table. I prepared for meetings as if decisions would be made there, not realizing that the men had aligned prior to the meeting on the path they wanted to pursue. It turned out that the meeting itself was really a formality, not a step in the decision-making process. I quickly realized I needed to build the case for anything I wanted to do well in advance of pitching it in a meeting. I reached out to colleagues in HR, IT, and finance and brought them along for support. When I was grilled in a meeting, I had the additional perspectives that could help clarify and support my initiatives.

You must understand how decisions are made, and you must embrace that process—whatever it may be in your organization. If it's all driven by money, then you need people from finance on your side. If HR has a lot of power, get them on board. If you're servicing a certain group of stakeholders, such as franchisees or engineers, align with them. Understand their perspectives and pain points, and figure out how they can be influencers when strategic decisions come up. Identify your barriers, both systemically and on specific initiatives. Address those barriers as early as possible so they don't have the opportunity to surprise you later on. Understand the formal and informal ways that things get done. Oftentimes the meeting does not actually happen in the meeting room. Perhaps you will never get onto your CEO's calendar without first reaching out to her admin. Your ability to navigate internal politics is an important part of operating as a strategic leader.

When forging these new relationships, being able to tell good stories is a powerful enabler. Ensure your stories are backed up with relevant, credible data. Show people what the future could be and how you can make their jobs/lives easier. If you can paint a brilliant and believable picture of a better future state, people will want to go there with you. Here's an example, via Taylor and Sam. Both are in a situation where they've recognized the need for an unpopular change and are trying to acquire allies.

> **Taylor**
> We trained 1,674 first-level supervisors last month, and 72 percent of them have already turned over. Yet 96 percent of them gave five-star ratings to the instructor, Magda. Everybody loves Magda. But we need to find another spot for her because of the high turnover. That population in the first-level supervisor job role has always turned over at a really high rate, so we should stop investing so much training in them. For the ones that get promoted, we can do catch-up training later. You with me?

> **Sam**
> First-level supervisor turnover has long been a pain point for us, and I have an idea about how we can bring it down. Right now we're focusing intense, centralized training efforts on this population. What if we instead equip their managers to provide coaching and mentoring right on the job? We've heard from our first-level supervisors that they

> feel unsupported in a very demanding role, which points to a need for a stronger manager presence. I'm proposing a fresh and unique program that uses a mobile simulation to teach coaching skills in a modular, bite-sized fashion. Our managers are already busy, so they can jump into the simulation on their iPads when they have an extra five minutes and aren't being taken away from their teams for yet more training time. The training would take an average of one month for a manager to complete; if we can reduce first-level supervisor turnover by even 5 percent in the following month, the training program will have paid for itself.

Who would you back? Notice that Taylor peppers you with numbers, but they're out of context. If you don't have a learning background, do you have any idea what she's talking about? Sam's approach is actually not number-heavy, but her argument is constructed from the data she knows the business cares about (and she would be able to rattle off the numbers if pressed). She's also gone outside of her silo, surveying the first-level supervisors to find out what they need on the job. Further, Taylor is pointing out a problem that everybody already knows exists, while Sam is offering a solution. And Sam has given you her metric for success: reducing turnover by 5–8 percent will cover the costs of her initiative, and her colleagues are well acquainted with the cost-savings potential of bringing down turnover. Sam knows who she is speaking to and shows that she understands what's important to them. Sam stuck her neck out and committed to a number. She was smart to give a range because that gives her some wiggle room. Even if Sam is off target a little bit, it will be easier to manage because she framed her argument in a way that people could understand.

What about the bullies?

Let's face it: just because you aren't in high school anymore doesn't mean that you won't encounter people who act like they still are. A California-based law firm has a granite plaque to remind everybody to be nice. "The gray slab, displayed in the law firm's reception area, proclaims that employees always say please and thank you, welcome feedback, and acknowledge the contributions of others."[16] Yes, this is really present in an adult, professional office. A longtime partner at the firm is quoted in the Wall Street Journal as saying that the rules "serve as a daily reminder to keep things civil at work."[17]

In your professional life, these bullies, barriers, and naysayers are the first people you need to address. You can't be the strategic leader of a winning organization and be non-confrontational. Find ways to strengthen your ability to deal with disagreements. When you find yourself stuck in a disagreement, start a new conversation with the other party and go into it ready to listen to his or her point of view. You're not trying to win the argument. You're trying to defuse the situation and find a middle ground that is amenable to both parties. When we talk about winning in a conflict situation, we mean that you come up with a solution where both sides feel like they've won. When the discussion becomes tense, don't run away. Stay in the conversation and encourage open dialogue. You will always have people who disagree with you, but in so many cases, if you allow them to feel heard, the conflict goes away. Don't assume they're out to get you, and don't take it personally. Truly hear and understand the other party's point of view. When necessary, be equipped with facts and data that support your point of view.

How to Report on Data, Trends, and Findings

When you're making a formal presentation or preparing a report, use the headlining approach to sharing what you've learned—put the good stuff up front and include the nitty gritty later, where anyone who wants it can find it. Even though you aren't engaging in dialogue as you would when speaking with executives, your written reports and presentations must quickly home in on what's important to your audience. Here are examples of how Taylor and Sam open the same presentation answering a stakeholder's critical business question: Was the time hourly employees spent away from the job for a training program worth it for store profitability?

16 https://www.wsj.com/articles/companies-wake-up-to-the-problem-of-bullies-at-work-1510758000

17 Ibid.

Taylor

So, we looked at stores where the hourly employees completed the training, and we compared their sales in the month after training to the same month in stores in similar markets where employees didn't get any training at all. Looking at stores in similar markets allowed us to control for things like a seasonal dip in sales, which we typically see at this time of the year anyway, but we were able to factor that out in our regression analysis and get down to whether the training was really responsible for any change in sales whatsoever. Now, it costs us $27.64 per hour, per employee, just to take people off the floor, because not only do we have to pay their wage while they're training, but we also have to pay for someone else to be there to cover their station. And that doesn't even include the cost to build and deliver the training! So when you add that up at an average of twenty employees per store, across the seventeen stores in the region that have received training so far, and then multiply by the three total hours it takes to complete the training—which includes two and a half hours of training plus breaks, plus time to get in and out of the training room and log in and ask questions and all that extra stuff, so three hours is probably a conservative estimate on how long it actually takes—anyway, it's pretty expensive to put these people through training! And that's why we are looking for an ROI before rolling the program out to all stores across the country. Any questions so far?

Sam

Last month, our regional managers asked whether the time their hourly employees spent in training was really worth taking them away from the sales floor. The answer to that question is yes. Stores that have adopted the new training program have experienced a 10% lift in sales compared to stores in similar markets that haven't adopted the program. At a time of the year when our sales are typically soft, this impressive increase shows that we need to roll out the training program in all stores across the country.

Now, Taylor is providing a lot of useful and important data here—data that absolutely need to be included in a formal report. However, she has completely missed the opportunity to answer the question the stakeholders asked. Surely she's lost them by now. These stakeholders know it's expensive to send people to training—that's why they asked the question in the first place! Your report should answer their question right up front, and then unpack the relevant data later on. Don't make your readers wade through pages of formulas and data to get to what they really want to know.

Quick and Dirty Takeaways on Communication

- **Begin by knowing yourself.** Once you know how you tend to communicate, you can work on emphasizing your strengths and compensating for your weaknesses. Take the time to record yourself—you may not be coming across the way you think! A mentor or colleague who will give honest feedback is invaluable here.
- **Next, know your audience.** How well you can know them will vary depending on the situation, but do what you can to determine what they care about and how they prefer to receive information.
- **Communicate with intention.** Even small, unplanned, informal interactions can have an intention. Know what you need to get across and stay focused on that. Don't waste opportunities with key leaders, and don't talk about being too busy. You're calm and in control!
- **Give the headlines and let your audience follow up.** Entice them with the big finding or important information. Once you've captured their attention, you can go into the details as needed.
- **Be aware of feedback.** If your audience is glazing over or seems distracted, you need to change something up! Ask probing questions and make sure they're following along with you.
- **Practice makes perfect.** Use video so you can see yourself the way others see you. Trusted friends and colleagues can also be a great source for feedback on your communication.

Checklist for Factor 1: Develop Your Foundational Skills

- ☐ Do you understand the big picture of your organization, as well as your place in it?
- ☐ Are you knowledgeable about what's going on inside and outside of your organization?
- ☐ Do you set time aside for strategic thinking?
- ☐ Do you have the executive presence of a strategic leader?
- ☐ Are you accountable for your actions?
- ☐ Does your calendar work for you?
- ☐ Do you have a vision for your career and life?
- ☐ Do you have a personal development board of stakeholders committed to your success?
- ☐ Are you communicating like a strategic leader by connecting to your audience, thinking about your messaging, and sharing the right amount of detail?
- ☐ Do you listen with the intent to hear, with an understanding of both words and body language?

FACTOR 1: Develop your foundational skills

Figure 4.1

Chapter 5

Factor 2—Establish the Vision

Before we jump into *how* you go about crafting your function or department's vision and strategy, let's talk about what these words mean at a higher level. A lot of people use terms like vision, strategy, goals, mission, plan, and objectives interchangeably. They are all part of strategic planning. Here is what we mean by vision, mission, and strategy:

Vision (the *why*): Tag line or overarching description of your company's ideal state. It's generally timeless and considered a blue-sky approach. The vision is the reason you are in business and typically doesn't change, at least not often. Most visions aren't directly measurable.

Sample vision statements:

- Disney: To make people happy.
- Google: To organize the world's information and make it universally accessible and useful.
- Instagram: Capture and share the world's moments.

Mission (the *what* and *why*): Describes why you are doing what you do. The mission statement highlights the business you are currently in and the customer needs you are trying to meet. The mission is action-oriented and forward-thinking. It's not lofty like the vision and is starting to get more concrete. The mission may be modified over time.

Sample mission statements:

- Microsoft: To help people around the world realize their full potential.
- Starbucks: To inspire and nurture the human spirit—one person, one cup, and one neighborhood at a time.
- Target: Our mission is to make Target your preferred shopping destination in all channels by delivering outstanding value, continuous innovation and exceptional guest experiences by consistently fulfilling our Brand Promise: Expect More. Pay Less.®

Strategy (the *how*): High-level plan that includes short- and long-term goals for driving the mission to realize the vision. The strategy changes and evolves over time. Some organizations update their strategies each year, others do so less frequently. It's not unheard of to have to update strategies rapidly when a crisis occurs. In business, there is a company-wide strategy that trickles down to functional or departmental strategies. Strategies include goals, so ideally they are more directly measurable than the mission and vision. The idea is that if you're meeting your strategic goals, then you're supporting the mission of the business to achieve your vision.

For-profit companies don't publicly share their strategic plans due to competitive advantage. Nonprofit and government agencies often do share theirs because they are accountable to outside funders, donors, and citizens for their performance.

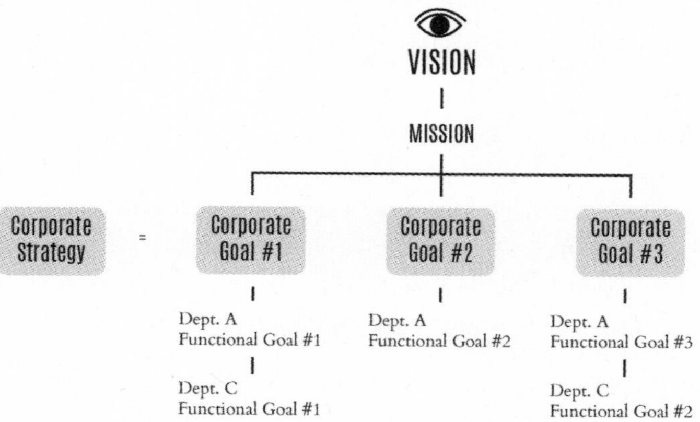

Figure 5.1

The point is, they are all parts of strategic planning that are linked together to realize the ultimate vision. When you hear someone talk about the big picture, this is a big part of what they mean. The vision, mission, and strategy frame the organization, and how the company is performing against high-level goals, as well as in the context of the industry and marketplace happenings, fill in the big picture.

Here is an example of the strategic direction for a hypothetical baby store.

Vision: Be the world's best baby supply store.

Mission: Provide our customers with a one-stop shop for all their baby needs.

Strategy:

- Increase global revenue by 25 percent
- Form retail partnerships with the world's leading baby brands
- Seek out up-and-coming brands and niche products to offer fresh and exciting new items in our stores
- Staff our locations with knowledgeable and friendly retail associates who will be every new parent's best friend
- Evaluate overall product offerings to ensure we don't have any gaps and truly are a one-stop shop
- Open an additional ten locations in major metropolitan areas

Corporate Vision:	Be the world's best baby supply store
Corporate Mission:	Provide our customers with a one-stop shop for all their baby needs.
Corporate Strategy:	**Goals** • Increase the global revenue by 25% • Form retail partnerships with the world's leading baby brands • Seek out up-and-coming brands and niche products to offer fresh and exciting new products in our stores • Staff our locations with knowledgeable and friendly retail associates who will be every new parent's best friend • Open an additional 10 locations in major global metropolitan areas • Evaluate overall product offerings to ensure we don't have any gaps and truly are a one-stop shop

Figure 5.2

You can see how these statements become progressively more tactical. This example corporate strategy is still very high level, but you can begin to see how various functions or departments can work on different components of the strategy. If your team is responsible for scouting real estate and opening new locations, then you have your marching orders for the year. But what if you're in a department that isn't given a specific task in the strategy? Then it's up to you to determine where your support is needed. For example, if you're in IT, you'll play a significant role in opening new locations while keeping all employees connected and productive. If you are in human resources, you need to be sure your organization has the right people in the right roles to achieve the strategic goals.

It's also worth noting that the strategy becomes measurable. The vision is a highly subjective statement; you can imagine many brands putting forth evidence to support the claim that they offer the world's best baby supply store, but there aren't inherent metrics for determining who can rightly claim that title. Is it the brand with the highest gross sales? Highest foot traffic? Strongest online sales? Most social media followers? Highest online star rating? Each brand would likely highlight its strongest metric and call itself the leader. The mission moves toward the quantifiable, but it would take a great deal of mental acrobatics to determine success metrics for being the one-stop shop for all baby needs. Is that made up of the number of products offered? Revenue growth? Number of knowledgeable, competent store associates? Number of retail locations? Variety of delivery options? It's still pretty subjective: one parent's one-stop shop may be another parent's overwhelming nightmare.

The sample strategy has six statements that are concrete and measurable, and they will drive you to the *how*. An internet search can help you identify the world's leading baby brands. There could be a target number of up-and-coming brands to partner with in order to give buyers an attainable goal for the year. Buyers could also evaluate how many products the store offers that aren't available in competing stores. The learning department can measure the knowledge and performance of retail associates, and customer satisfaction scores can show whether new parents feel like the retail associates are helpful. The final strategy statement provides its own success metric (10 new stores).

This chapter started with corporate strategy because that's where each department or function's strategy begins. Some leaders help construct the corporate strategy, and others are responsible for constructing a strategy for their individual functions or departments. No matter what role you play, you need to be aware of all levels of the corporate vision and strategy, as well as the ways your functional strategy supports corporate's. We use the term corporate to refer to the overarching strategy at the top of the business, and functional strategy refers to a strategy covering one specific part of the business. Your organization may have a different structure, but there is most likely one strategy covering everybody, and then more detailed (or perhaps informal) strategies covering specific people or groups.

Diana

I believe a strong vision is one of the most powerful enablers of success. At McDonald's our company's vision was: We are our customers' favorite place and way to eat and drink. This was a customer-centered vision that our top leaders continually referenced and kept us focused on. My team was responsible for developing and delivering the training and tools that enabled our people to deliver on the corporate vision. Our role in bringing that customer vision to life was our functional vision: We develop top talent, create the best environment, do the most important work, and achieve world-class execution and results for the system.

As a leader, I continued to cast and recast the vision to ensure every team member understood, supported, and was engaged in the right activities to achieve our vision. I knew that in order to make this happen, we needed every team member to embrace the vision and help bring it to life. When we first created and adopted this vision, we did the exercise of having each person come up with their top two core values and then share with their fellow team members how those values tied into our vision. It was so inspiring to hear my team members' answers, and the exercise helped people commit even more to bringing our vision to life. We also used our team vision as part of the hiring process to bring in people whose competencies aligned with the vision. As part of orientation for new team members, we would cover our vision and do this same exercise with our new hires, so from the very beginning they understood our vision.

Here's another example to illustrate, using our friends Sam and Taylor. As the tactical leader at our hypothetical baby supply store, Taylor comes up with the following vision and strategy for the learning department:

> **Vision:** Create the most engaging, cutting-edge training programs at every level of the organization.
>
> **Strategy:**
>
> - Touch every manager with a new leadership development program
> - Get at least 60 percent of employees to participate in a social learning platform
> - Overhaul compliance training to make it more engaging and available on popular mobile platforms

From a training perspective, Taylor's vision and strategy seem admirable. The problem is that Taylor's vision and strategy are connected to each other, but they aren't connected to the corporate vision and strategy given above. You could argue for Taylor's vision contributing to the corporate vision of being the leading baby supply store, but even the language in the vision feels disconnected from the business. It emphasizes learner engagement in training programs—a vanity metric that should instead point to an activity metric, like performance on the job—and being at the forefront of trends in professional training. Trends are important when they can serve the corporate strategy, but following trends for the sake of trendiness is a road to nowhere. Nothing about Taylor's strategy supports the four corporate goals for the year. Developing leaders is a worthy goal, but it's hard to see how Taylor would connect that back to anything corporate is focusing on. The social learning platform also seems tangential, and nothing in the corporate strategy indicated a need for new compliance training.

Here is Sam's vision and strategy:

> **Vision:** Create a skilled and competent workforce for the world's best baby supply store.
>
> **Strategy:**
>
> - Equip new retail associates to be every parent's best friend by overhauling our onboarding training and offering support during the associate's first ninety days on the job
> - Ensure existing associates are touched by ongoing development efforts at least once every other month
> - Attract and develop the industry's best buyers with training, tools, and internal support

Right away, you can see that Sam is tuned into the corporate vision. Her learning department vision echoes the language used in the corporate vision: if the brand will be the world's best baby supply store, she is developing the workforce to achieve that ideal. Her strategy points tie to several of the corporate strategy goals, building that "new parent's best friend" persona that corporate wants its associates to embody and supporting the opening of new locations with strong onboarding. Her idea of offering development programs for existing associates ensures those who've had a longer tenure with the company will embrace and model the new ideals. She also recognizes the need to support the company's buyers, and you can easily imagine her meeting with them to find out what they need in order to find those up-and-coming baby brands.

Both Taylor and Sam created strategies whose impact could be measured, but notice that Taylor's goals can be easily assessed with internal learning department data—they aren't measured by business results. Some of Sam's goals will require learning department data, but they also need disparate data such as employee and store performance data if she is going to accurately assess the effectiveness of the programs she proposes. As a result, Sam will have more leading indicators and hard proof of success that demonstrates achievement of the corporate strategy.

In modern business, change is a reality and a requirement. What happens to your functional strategy if the corporate strategy changes? It changes, too. The main rule is communicate and clarify. Be transparent; explain why something needs to change, and make every effort to understand the required change. Explain to your team what is taking place from the corporate strategy down to your functional strategy, and make sure they feel supported. Be accountable and transparent to build trust and show leadership. During times of change, you have an opportunity to shine as a strategic leader.

The Visioning Process

Now that we've defined the functional vision and strategy, we're going to talk about the process for coming up with these seminal documents. In chapter 2, we went into great detail about how to understand where your business is and where it's going. You absolutely must understand this if you hope to have a vision and strategy that will move the business forward. Further, by understanding your business, it's far easier to focus your vision and strategy. Without the business landscape, you are essentially visioning in a vacuum. If you've ever found yourself at the beginning of any project without parameters, you know how difficult this can be. Imagine sitting down to write a novel and staring at the blank page, the immense pressure to come up with the perfect opening line weighing on your soul. If you don't even know what your novel is going to be about, how can you possibly invent something that will grip every reader who happens to flip open your book in a bookstore?

When you understand where your business is and where it's going, you also understand the opportunities for your function. Your most important purpose is bringing the company's goals to life via your expertise and areas of reach. The learning department's vision in our baby store example is to develop the workforce of the world's best baby store, because the corporate vision is to BE the world's best baby store. These visions are aligned, and if the learning department's strategy is supporting its vision, then the strategy will fall right into line with the corporate strategy.

Keep in mind that logic makes you think while emotions make you act.

Visions can vary widely depending upon the business. If you work for a well-loved consumer brand, perhaps your vision is tied to protecting said brand while also sustaining growth. Your task is to create the vision and then bring it to life for your team. Remind them of it every time you meet. Regardless of what exactly the vision is, it should empower your team with a sense of purpose. Hopefully it helps them to feel engaged and energized, too. The vision should give all of you a sense of purpose for everything you do. Keep in mind that logic makes you think while emotions make you act. Get your team logically and emotionally engaged to keep them energized.

Strategizing

Once the vision is in place, it's time to build a more concrete picture of where you're going. What's the plan? What does the future state look like? For many organizations, a new strategy is developed annually, and we are going to assume that timetable for the purposes of our example. If your strategy follows the calendar year, what do you hope to achieve by December 31 or by the end of your fiscal year? There's nothing to stop you from developing a multi-year strategy, so don't restrict yourself to what you can accomplish in a year.

When you jump into the strategizing process, you aren't going to work alone. Begin by working with your own team before taking the strategy out to stakeholders in other business units and corporate leadership. In the next chapter you'll learn about creating a governance board, and their support can be invaluable in defining your strategy. If your team is on the smaller side, you may find yourself involving everyone in the initial planning and brainstorming meetings. For larger groups, it may make more sense to limit participation to those at the manager level and above. Your goal here is to gain the buy-in of your entire team. Perhaps you solicit suggestions from the whole department, and then you review those and refine with your managers. Then you go back to the larger group to show them what you've come up with, allowing them to refine through a few iterations. You're not necessarily looking for a consensus, but you're consulting with your team to find out what you may have left out and what they think is important when it comes to realizing the vision.

As you create the future state, you'll likely find yourself doing an inventory of the current state, which just so happens to be the next step in the process. If you like to work visually, put your future state on the right and your current state on the left. The space in between will be filled with the things you need to do to move from left to right. As you understand the process of going from the current state to the future state, you'll find yourself making changes. What is realistic? What needs to happen first? What fits into the budget? What will your stakeholders support? What skill sets do you have on your team? What skill sets do you need to achieve your strategic goals?

As a director for the learning department, here is Sam's strategy, using the baby store example from above. Remember her strategic goals:

- Equip new retail associates to be every parent's best friend by overhauling our onboarding training and offering support during the associate's first ninety days on the job
- Ensure existing associates are touched by ongoing development efforts at least once every other month
- Attract and develop the industry's best buyers with training, tools, and internal support

Current state	Needs *(gaps between current state and future state)*	Future state
Current onboarding is piecemeal; each store does things differently and has various pieces of legacy training on hand. Current onboarding ends after the first 30 days of employment. Product knowledge trainnig is strong for new hires but doesn't offer resources for existing employees when we add new products.	• Compile and streamline current onboarding materials. • Determine what new hires need in days 31-90. • Develop a social platform to foster peer support during the first 90 days. • Create ongoing product knowledge training for all retail associates that can be updated as we add new products to the store.	Equip new retail associates to be every parent's best friend by overhauling our onboarding training and offering support during the associate's first 90 days on the job.
Existing associates average six months between development efforts, and those efforts are primarily focused on compliance and systems training. We have very little available soft skill development.	• Determine gaps in existing associate training; how can we better serve their needs? Interview/survey associates and their managers. • Create new opportunities for informal training that don't require extensive development resources but still offer regular development opportunities for associates.	Ensure existing associates are touched by ongoing development efforts at least once every other month.
Our portfolio does not currently contain any skills training for buyers.	• Sit with the buyer team leads to find out what they need and how we can support them (this has never been done!). • Benchmark against other retail buyer training to find out what we should be offering.	Attract and develop the industry's best buyers with training, tools, and internal support.

Figure 5.3

Sam's strategy is ambitious! She is overhauling a large and costly legacy program, and she's also reaching out to colleagues she hasn't partnered with in the past. At this point, it's a good time for Sam to begin socializing her strategy outside of her function. Again, she is not looking to gain consensus from every single stakeholder and business leader, but to get their input for consideration. She's also doing some early-stage marketing of her strategy; you want people to be aligned with what you're doing, not surprised to learn of your priorities. Help them feel like they are a part of it.

A note here: it's important not to iterate forever. When you present to your colleagues, you're not asking them for a complete rewrite, and it's important not to give them the impression that they should feel compelled to do one. Show them what you've come up with, and ask if there's anything major you've overlooked. Ask if they think you need to review certain aspects. You're not asking for their adoption or sign-off; be careful not to make them think you absolutely will incorporate their feedback. You may not! This is the difference between a consultative decision-making process and a consensus. Don't look for consensus on your strategy: you are highly unlikely to get one and attempting to do so will stop you from moving forward. Make your reviewers feel positive about the opportunity to review and let you know if you're on the right track.

Even if you aren't one-hundred percent certain that everything is perfect, move forward; it's preferable to doing nothing.

When you get to the point that the items in the "Needs" column match up with your available funding, it's time to stop iterating and begin your work. Trust your gut to tell you the strategy is ready to be put into action. There's always the danger of falling into planning paralysis. Even if you aren't one-hundred percent certain that everything is perfect, move forward; it's preferable to doing nothing. Remember, this is a living document! You want to be grounded in the needs of your stakeholders, but you must also have the flexibility to evolve as conditions dictate. Also, your individual teams need time for their own planning, as they will have their own micro-strategies based on the larger strategy. Everyone on your team should have some part of the strategy they can work on or influence. If you look at the needs in Sam's strategy, you can begin to envision how the various groups within her department will build out their action plans and tasks. Make sure they can hit the ground running, with budgets set, on the first business day of the year. While your timing may vary, we typically see organizations spend up to three months on functional strategic planning.

I don't know my desired state

Our example above had clear goals, but not every organization has such a concrete strategy and tight goals. Sometimes corporate strategies are much more vague, or even undocumented—it sits in a leader's brain and never gets clearly communicated. That makes it difficult to find your place to jump in. If that's your situation, you can network, ask questions, and document the strategy for yourself and your team so you have a clear line of sight to the vision. Otherwise, you'll find yourself guessing at where to go and what to do, hoping you hit some undefined target.

What if your business has a vague strategic statement, such as, "Sharpen our competitive edge," with no underlying goals? This could lead you in any number of directions, and it's likely to have a variety of meanings depending on what you talk to within the organization. Start by asking the leaders who drafted the vague strategy. What do they see as the goals? What gaps did they see in the organization or in the industry that needed to be closed? If you don't have access to higher level leaders, then ask around in your peer network. No matter what, don't guess at what they mean or what they want, because you may head down the wrong path. If you don't have adequate access, start by drafting a strategic plan for your own function and shopping it around to start the conversation internally. Sometimes it's easier for people to respond and react to something documented rather than a fuzzy discussion. This is where you leverage your political capital and start building more capital. Don't worry about being right or wrong. The goal is to build your strategy or plan to head down the right path.

How Will You Know If You've Succeeded?

As you build your functional strategy, including your goals, think about how each piece is measurable. For each strategic goal, you need business performance goals with mutually agreed-upon targets. Performance goals with accepted targets prevent disagreement over when a goal is reached. You either hit the target, miss the target, or come close. You need to know how you are doing along the way. For example, "Sharpen our competitive edge" is a great example of a strategic goal that doesn't seem measurable on its face. If you need direction on how to achieve this goal, you could ask yourself and your stakeholders these questions to determine what you need to measure.

- What does your industry look like or what happens to the industry when you sharpen your competitive edge?
- What does your organization look like when you sharpen the competitive edge?
- What do the functional departments need to sharpen the organization's competitive edge?

Say this was the strategy for the baby store. Sam spoke with her leadership and determined that to sharpen the competitive edge means to drive the industry toward more environmentally friendly practices. We need to drive environmentally friendly practices because there is a greater customer demand for green products. Now she has a more concrete way to sharpen the store's competitive edge. She plans to procure partners who adhere to green practices and cut out any partners who do not. Making this green shift known to the industry and partner network will initiate the desired change. Now, what do the individual departments of the baby store need to do to focus on the shift to green practices? First, each department needs to be sure they are compliant with green practices internally. Then they need to hold their peers accountable to green practices. They need to deliver solutions that are in alignment with green practices. All of these efforts to move toward green practices will drive the organization toward achieving its goal of sharpening our competitive edge. All of these actions taken to build greener practices can be measured.

Do you see how the strategy is driving the measurement, not the other way around? In a later chapter, we show you how to build an Impact Blueprint that graphically links your measurement strategy to your corporate strategy.

Quick and Dirty Takeaways for Factor 2

Here are some key points to remember as you set your direction.

- **A winning function's vision and strategy are closely linked to corporate strategy.** Make sure everyone on your team understands how their work drives business performance. Your most important purpose is bringing the company's vision to life via your expertise and areas of reach.
- **As you develop your strategy, share it and solicit feedback, but don't iterate forever.** You are highly unlikely to reach a consensus with everyone involved, and attempting to do so will stop you from moving forward.
- **If you're not sure what your strategy should be, start by looking inside and outside the organization.** Find out what internal expectations there are, and determine what other winning organizations are doing. Can you adapt their best practices to fit your own organization?
- **Make each component measurable.** Make sure everyone has a clear understanding of the definition of success.

Checklist for Factor 2: Establish the vision

- ☐ Have you created a well-defined vision and strategy for your function?
- ☐ Are your function's vision and strategy aligned to the broader organization's vision and strategy?
- ☐ Is your strategy concrete and measurable?
- ☐ Does everyone on your team understand the vision and current strategy, and is each team member able to explain them?
- ☐ Does everyone on your team know how their work aligns with the business and higher vision?

Figure 5.4

Chapter 6

Factor 3—Engage Stakeholders

Are you feeling strategic yet? In this chapter, you'll start looking out from yourself and on to the people around you—specifically, the other leaders and stakeholders who are impacted by your work. You will learn how to collaborate with your peers, and also how to learn from them. Remember when we talked about accountability in chapter 2? Through this process of leveraging stakeholders, you will build a culture of accountability and a network of supporters throughout your organization.

If you've been around a larger company for a while, you're probably familiar with the concept of a functional governance board. These can look different depending on the function and the culture, but generally a governance board is a group of stakeholders either from within or outside the organization that collaborates with the function's leadership and has a stake in the function's success. Strategic leaders welcome this collaboration, and they also know how to manage a balance between what the stakeholders want and what's best for the organization.

The Governance Board

Regardless of the size or type of your organization, we recommend that you have a set of internal and external (if appropriate) organizational advisors for your department or function who can offer a view of the big picture, help you step over landmines, and prepare you for the future. An active, supportive governance board is a success factor for strategic leaders running a winning function. As an up-and-coming leader, you may be asked to serve on a governance board, which is an excellent opportunity for personal development, networking, and building political capital. When you become the leader of a function, you'll want to establish your own governance board. Even as the strategic leader looking out over the jungle, you are still limited by what you can see. A governance board gives you insights from people who can help guide your leadership because they also have a vested interest in the company's direction overall.

The board comprises people from within or outside of the organization who collaborate with departmental leadership and have a stake in your success. They help you to make hard decisions, and they'll also lend their credibility to your strategy and decisions. They'll vet and fine-tune your vision and strategy. And most importantly, they bring the outside perspective you're lacking.

You may have heard terms like governing board, working board, advisory board, or executive board. The primary differences are:

- Governing boards set initial direction and have full authority to act in the owners' best interests. Governing boards function at arm's length from the operational organization. They focus on the big picture, are future-oriented, and act as a single entity.
- Working boards lead the department or organization but also do double duty as staff. Working boards often get caught up in project management and set aside the governing function.
- Advisory boards provide insight and perspective to any decision maker, including boards. An advisory board typically does not have authority of its own but works to educate some person or body.[18]

What will the governance board do?

The purpose of your governance board will depend upon the maturity of your function, but a primary goal is to ensure you add value to the business in meaningful ways. Just as you did with your personal board to help with your career development (see chapter 3), your functional governance board helps with your function's development and growth. Think about what you want the board to help you accomplish and clearly lay out those goals from the start. In general, these people are going to help you make better decisions and navigate the politics of organizational systems. They'll give you feedback on your strategy and any decisions you make, and they will also be advocates for you when you ask for funding or need support in general. They will help you set targets to hit and track your progress toward those targets, which reinforces a culture

18 http://www.policygovernanceconsulting.com/about-governance-and-board-work/different-types-of-boards

of accountability (lots more about how you do that in the coming chapters). A governance board should also present information you may not otherwise be aware of; each member brings a new perspective. They can help you to understand how what you do impacts them, and how their functions can support your efforts. When it comes to being strategic, your governance board is an invaluable resource.

Some functional governance boards have a stronger decision-making role and are responsible for sign-off on decisions. We prefer that you maintain the control and have a more consultative model, as well as an agile structure. While you want the board's guidance, you don't want to slow down the pace of business and create a frustrating layer of bureaucracy. It's important to decide at the outset what types of decisions the governance board will be involved in and what your function will handle internally. When you onboard new governance board members, provide a clear description of their roles, responsibilities, their purpose, and the scope of their involvement. You want board members to have some skin in the game, so to speak, because it helps to keep them engaged. Their feedback needs to make an impact. As you get started, ask your governance board how your function adds value to the business, as well as how it aligns with the business mission and vision.

If you are leading a large corporate function, we recommend that you have a formal governance board. A formally established board ensures member commitment and participation, and it also ensures that you prioritize your goals. If you fear that you do not have the political capital to start a formal governance board, you can start one with just a few people and grow as the board becomes more influential.

> **Diana**
> My governance board was indispensable when I was VP of learning and development at McDonald's, responsible for the development and deployment of the training and resources for the restaurants and those who supported or oversaw them. Here is the mission we used to give structure to the governance board:

> As champions of the connection between training and improved business results, we provide leadership that guides McDonald's Training, Learning, and Development. Through feedback, review, and piloting, the team shapes curriculum and tools to meet the expected outcomes. We will act as catalysts for change to achieve expected outcomes.

We had criteria or screens we used on who should be on the governance board from our field (those who operated restaurants) since that was our key audience, such as maintaining an acceptable level of performance and being supported by the officer in charge of their area or function.

We defined roles and responsibilities of our field members such as:

- Participate in team calls and pilot / test curriculum and tools
- Provide feedback on the curriculum and tools
- Solicit feedback from their peers and share it with full board at least one time per quarter
- Be a champion and advocate for the training curriculum and tools

How do you establish the governance board charter?

The charter formally outlines the mission and activities of the board, membership requirements, member terms, and roles. You charter doesn't need to be a big legal document; a working document to provide your board with structure and rules of engagement will suffice. We recommend the following components:

- **Objectives:** Identify, at a high level, what you are trying to accomplish with the board. The objectives should be stated in a manner that is easy to relate to.
- **Scope:** Describe the boundaries of work along the dimensions of geography/location, users, organizations, functions, technology, areas involved in defining scope,

etc. Additionally, identify what is NOT in the boundaries due to timing, limitations, etc.

- **Roles and responsibilities:** Outline specific roles and responsibilities to ensure member alignment.
- **Resource requirements:** Indicate any resources that need to be allocated to successfully run the board, such as meeting support and materials that are critical to this project.
- **Members:** List all the team members and indicate whether there are term limits.
- **Critical success measurements:** Describe the factors that will determine if the board is successful.
- **Activities, duties, and responsibilities:** This section is the meat and bones of the committee's charter. It spells out exactly what the committee needs to do. More importantly, it outlines what the committee is responsible for. For example, a duty of the governance committee may be to recruit new members and bring candidates to the board for review.

Who are your stakeholders?

Your governance board is made up of stakeholders who represent a 360-degree view of everyone who touches (or is touched by) your work. It's everyone who has a stake in what you do, what you deliver, and where you're going. At the strategic level you may identify stakeholders to help you build your governance board, and some may serve on the board. Other stakeholders may not participate in the governance board at all but may review or contribute to your department's goals and help you stay on track toward your goal. It is important to note that at a tactical level, individual projects will have their own stakeholders, depending upon the goals and the audience.

Here's an example of how stakeholders can make or break your work. Sam and Taylor work for a food manufacturing company, and the leaders have decided to launch a new product: a line of vegan snacks that are nutritious, portable, and tasty. Taylor is responsible for market research, so she begins by sharing samples with a few friends (one of whom is an actual vegan) and asking for their feedback. She also visits three grocery stores in her town to see what they offer in the vegan snack department. Finally, she googles "best vegan snacks" to read reviews on the most popular products.

Can you see how short-sighted Taylor's market research is? If she is creating a product for her friends, in her town, then perhaps she's off to a good start, but that's not the goal here. She is supposed to be launching a whole new line of vegan snacks, and her customer base is extremely narrow based on who is represented in her research. Sam approaches the task by putting together a marketing plan, and then surveying vegans across the country about their needs and preferences for snacks. She interviews major grocery chains to find out about regional differences in sales of vegan products. Like Taylor, she also looks at the best, most popular products already on the market, but goes further by investigating their ingredients to see how her new line can be different.

Sam represents a leader who consults with business stakeholders when building strategies. Taylor represents the leader who stays within her own silo for conducting business.

Whom should you invite to join your governance board?

Your governance board is a collaboration of decision makers and influencers inside your organization, and sometimes outside of your organization. The governance board members are right there in the jungle with you, looking over the treetops to make sure you're in the right jungle. In fact, they go a step further and look out across the trees in an entirely different direction, keeping you informed about things happening in other jungles.

In short, you want to include strategic, collaborative people who are at the highest levels of the organization, with whom you need strong alignment. The people involved in making decisions about your funding are important participants. They may be executive leaders or at the director level, depending on the size and structure of your organization. Some VPs will send a director to serve as his or her proxy, and serving on a governance board can be a great way to develop the leadership skills of an up-and-coming leader. If appropriate, you may include external customers, partners, vendors, suppliers, or anyone else who has their finger on the pulse of your industry. Many of the participants will be able to offer information about future plans that you may not otherwise be privy to and help you see where your function needs to go.

It's equally important to include your detractors on your governance board. You want people who are skeptical of what you do and will push back on your ideas and strategies. Don't shy away from potentially heated discussions; strive to understand why your detractors feel the way they do. Opening a dialogue with detractors serves to reduce heated discussions in the future. You may even win them over through a board position, but at the very least they will push you to see your work from a new perspective. Be careful not to confuse your detractors with naysayers or complainers—you want people whose disagreement will be productive and ultimately lead to better solutions.

Also look for people who have great personal power and influence, regardless of their level in the organization. We all have those vocal individuals in our organizations who are full of knowledge and can communicate persuasively and have a strategic mindset. They make wonderful allies. Your governance board members should challenge you, be honest, be unafraid to share important information you may not want to hear, and ultimately help you build a better future.

Shoot for about eight to twelve participants. A minimum of four to six is appropriate for a smaller organization, and any more than twelve could make your meetings too chaotic. When you invite board members, we recommend setting a term limit—about two years is typical, but smaller organizations may need to operate differently to ensure the right business units are continually represented. Cycling people on and off the board helps you to introduce fresh perspectives. In some organizations, there may be a reciprocal relationship involved in governance board participation. Perhaps you sit on someone else's board or committee. Look for ways that you can support your board members in their own priorities.

Sometimes there are governance board participants who aren't official board members. These could be subject matter experts from your own group, or other content areas where you require their knowledge and support. You may also have observers from your department join meetings—it's yet another opportunity to develop the leadership skills of your up-and-coming talent.

How do you onboard new governance board members?

When you bring on new governance board members, it's important to set their expectations for their participation in the governance board, and also to bring them up to speed on what the board is working on. Ask them to review the charter first. The first meeting for a new board member shouldn't require a rehashing of old subject matter—it's your responsibility to prepare him or her. Discuss the charter, list of current board members, previous and future activities, meeting expectations, and your success measures ahead of time. Encourage new members to be active participants right from the start. Also remind them that they are your eyes and ears around the business.

Who leads the governance board?

Your governance board will need a leader who schedules meetings, sets agendas, facilitates discussion, and maintains regular communication with the board members. Governance board leadership could be a great way for one of your rising leaders to develop his or her skills. Of course, you can lead your own board, or you may have an ally from another business function who would make a good leader.

The board leader is also responsible for ensuring all board members remain engaged with the task at hand and helping to identify board members who have become disengaged. Basic meeting etiquette can go a long way in this regard: for example, if someone hasn't spoken in a while, ask for his or her opinion. Consider the regular sources of dialogue and try to make sure everyone is involved. If applicable, help to educate board members who don't have a strong grasp of your discipline. It's also a good strategic practice to ask for meeting feedback for your continuous improvement efforts.

How frequently do you meet?

How often you meet is going to depend upon your purpose. As anyone who has tried to schedule a meeting with a crew of busy people knows, you will need to be flexible with your meeting schedule. Be open to moving your set time if that makes it easier for most people to attend. Meeting in person is ideal, but give people the option to call in if they need to. For virtual meetings, we prefer to use a meeting tool that includes video and allows you to see people's faces during discussions.

What happens during board meetings?

Be sure to have a clear agenda that is shared prior to the meeting. Don't be afraid to ask for pre-work in the agenda. If you need the board members to review a document prior to the meeting, make that request clear. They should appreciate that approach because it will expedite the actual gathering. Your agenda will naturally be dictated by the goals you set for your governance board.

To help jumpstart your thinking about the structure of the meetings, here is a sample agenda:

- Welcome and agenda (by meeting facilitator)
- Introduce any new members or guests
- Update results from decisions made in previous meetings
- Review a current high-level progress update of your function, using tools such as your Impact Blueprint, scorecard, success metrics, etc.
- Cover key topics and decisions that need to be made by the board
- Open discussion; any new business
- Plans for the time before the next meeting
- Close

How do you communicate before and between meetings?

You want to make the most of your meeting times, so send out a brief summary of the discussion points for people to review prior to the meeting itself. If you're tracking success metrics or using a departmental Impact Blueprint, share that data regularly. Make it easy for people to engage in the content and give you their feedback. And when you act on their feedback, tell them about it, even if it's just an informal note thanking someone for a great idea.

Once or twice a year, solicit feedback (and share your thoughts) about how the board is working. Ask board members for ideas about how make the board more functional.

Quick and Dirty Takeaways for Factor 3

- **An active, supportive governance board organizes your stakeholders and builds a culture of accountability.** You're all in this together!
- **Invite strategic, collaborative participants, and also your detractors.** Include people who haven't traditionally been your allies. This is an opportunity for you to hear their concerns and win them over to your side.
- **Whatever structure you choose for your governance board, make sure there is a structure in place.** Your board members are busy people, just like you! Make sure expectations are clear and meetings are productive.
- **Communicate regularly.** All of your stakeholders share a stake in your success. Keep them informed about what's going on.

Checklist for Factor 3: Engage Stakeholders

- ☐ Have you built a functional governance board of stakeholders to help guide and support your work?
- ☐ Are your stakeholders looking across the organization to help you see the opportunities and anticipate challenges?
- ☐ Have you fostered a culture of accountability on your governance board?

Figure 6.1

Chapter 7

Factor 4—Build Your Strategic Plan

Strategic planning is a phrase that gets thrown around a lot, but most uses boil down to documenting a plan for what you're going to do during the course of the year (or another selected timeframe). A strategic leader plans in alignment with what the business is trying to accomplish. Essentially, you look at where you are today and where you want to be tomorrow. How will you get from today to tomorrow? How will you know if you've succeeded? Up to this point, this book has focused on qualities of strategic leadership: what it is and how to become a strategic leader, identify stakeholders, and formalize a group of them to help elevate your leadership and the department's results. Now that we've laid the groundwork, it's time to get into the day-to-day parts: what are you going to do as a function, department, and leader? How do you identify activities, plan programs, and launch new initiatives that are connected to the vision and mission? Where should your focus be in order to show that you're aligned to the vision? How do you build a roadmap to get into the right jungle? You're looking, acting, and thinking like a strategic leader. Now you're going to work like one.

Factors 4, 5, and 6 give you a process and tools for planning and executing, all while working transparently, fostering a culture of accountability, and impacting the business in ways that matter.

Factor 4: Build your strategic plan

1. Determine which corporate goal(s) your function needs to support (these come from the strategy of the business, as outlined in the previous chapter).

2. Draft your functional goals in alignment with the corporate goal(s).

3. Decide what information you need to show you are impacting your functional goals, and ask the right business impact questions.

Create Your Impact Blueprint

1. Determine where you can impact business performance by pursuing your functional goals. What information do you need to answer your business impact questions?

2. Decide what investments and initiatives you need to undertake to impact the business performance. What do you need to do to make a change?

Factor 5: Execute your strategic plan

1. Take action by undertaking initiatives that will impact the business.

2. Track the impact of your initiatives and investments on your business performance. Where are you winning?

3. Determine the current status of your progress toward your desired impact. How much of an impact are you having?

4. Answer your business impact questions. Show which metrics you impacted to make a difference in the business.

Factor 6: Make decisions to win

1. Report your performance. Share the answers to your business impact questions.

2. Make decisions. Decide if you need to change, and if so, how to change.

3. Make changes. Take action on the decisions you make.

4. Continuously improve. Monitor the impact of your initiative and investments against your functional goals. If the business alters its goals, change your functional goals accordingly and continue to monitor.

Let's jump into Factor 4: Build your strategic plan. If your organization has a preferred strategic planning process or framework, you can certainly follow that approach.

Diana

One tool that I have used to help with strategic planning is a SWOT Analysis. It helps a leader and organization identify its internal strengths and weaknesses, as well as its external opportunities and threats. It's particularly helpful if you have a tendency to get stuck in your limited line of sight and will help you to see if you are in the right jungle.

Strengths

1. What does our company do best?
2. How are we exceeding our customers' expectations?
3. What do we do better than our competitors?

Weaknesses

1. What does our company not do well?
2. Where are we behind competitors or failing to meet our customers' expectations?
3. Where are we lacking results? Where aren't we satisfying our customers?

Opportunities

1. What changes do we see that would boost demand over the next 3-5 years?
2. What opportunities do we think will emerge as a result of what is going on in the market and economy?
3. What changes could occur in the future that would benefit our location or company?

Threats

1. What changes do we see that might hurt demand over the next 3-5 years?
2. What might threaten us as a result of what's going on in the market and economy?
3. What change could occur in the future that would hurt our company?

Figure 7.1

It doesn't matter what type of organization you're in—you need a strategic plan that will yield actionable insights. Within a culture of accountability, a strategic plan should include these basic components:

- Functional goals that are clearly linked to corporate goals
- Business performance measures that show you whether you are on track to win
- Targets and actual results
- Status on progress toward the functional goals

When you follow a clean process with clear reporting, it's easier to make decisions, take action quickly, and observe immediate changes.

Why is strategic planning important for your function?

The process of strategic planning within your department or function includes:

- Outlining the functional goals that align to corporate goals you can reasonably impact
- Setting targets and timeframes for meeting the goals
- Determining what work or projects to undertake
- Identifying who will do the work

A strategic plan is your detailed road map for the year (or however long it's designed to guide you). As with all maps, the strategic plan provides you with direction, focus, and boundaries within which to work and make decisions. With a plan, you don't have to guess what to do, wonder if you are doing the right things, or shoot at some vague target. It's easier to stay on track and get back on track if you happen to veer off. Your strategic plan guides even day-to-day decision-making, offering a clear line of sight to the big win.

Whom do you include in the strategic planning process?

Your governance board and stakeholders will be invaluable resources in the strategic planning process, whether they are collaborating with you to build the plan or vetting a plan you've drafted. Depending on your function and corporate structure, you may also invite review from others who aren't formally on your governance board but have deeper insights into the corporate strategy. Remember, as a strategic leader, you take a consultative approach when working with others, as opposed to seeking a clear consensus—the final decision is up to you. You may or may not implement their feedback, but you do need their perspective to inform your decision-making. Ultimately, it's up to you to determine who is appropriate to include, but don't fall into the temptation of creating a strategic plan in isolation or without leaving your own silo. Remember your commitment to accountability and transparency as a strategic leader.

Plan, Do, Study, Act

When it's time to get down to planning, tactical people start thinking about *how* they're going to accomplish a set of tasks, perhaps even with goals in mind. Strategic leaders start by assessing what they need to accomplish to meet their goals. To contextualize the planning process, we like the four-phase PDSA framework: Plan, Do, Study, Act.[19]

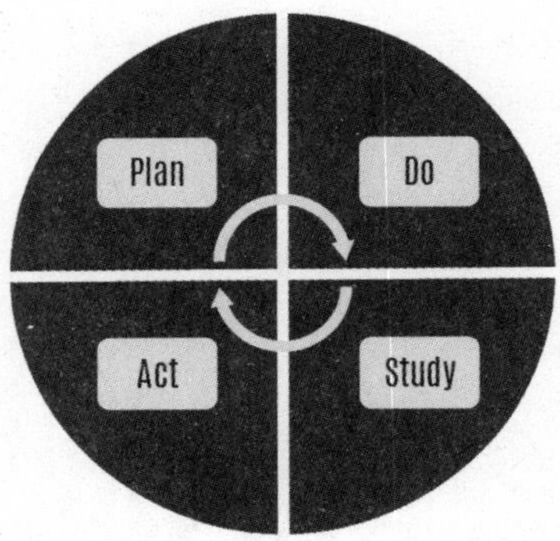

Figure 7.2

1. PLAN: collaboratively create your strategic plan. What are you going to do? Is it the right thing to do? How will you know you've done it? Ask the right business impact questions.

2. DO: execute your plan. When and how did or will you do it? Answer your business impact questions.

3. STUDY: interpret the answers to your business impact questions. Were the answers what you expected? Where should you stay the course? What changes will you have to make based on what you've learned? What decisions do you need to make to create your desired changes?

19 Moen, Nolan, and Provost. *Quality Improvement through Planned Experimentation.* New York: McGraw-Hill Education. 2012.

4. ACT: take action to make the desired change. Based on the evidence you have collected by answering your business impact questions, make decisions that will drive continuous organizational improvement.

The PDSA model is popular in healthcare, the U.S. federal government, education, and quality-focused organizations. It is a model designed to implement rapid change, and because it's cyclical, it leads to continuous improvement. The PDSA model is considered planned experimentation. You will consistently ask yourself, "What can we do and change in order to improve?" You apply the model continuously in order to always get better at what you're doing.

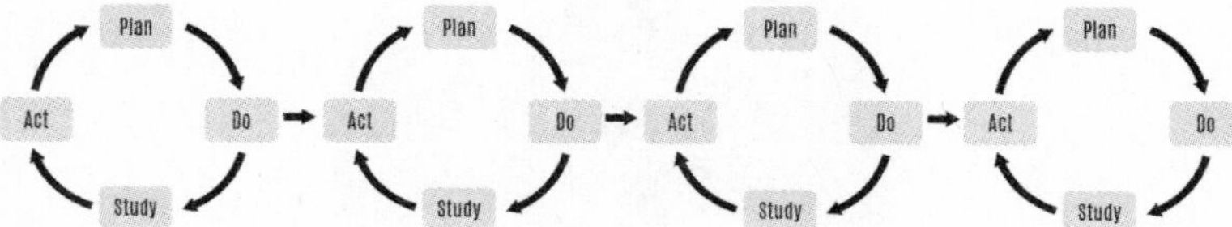

Figure 7.3

Many organizations use the PDSA process without realizing it. That is, they plan for work to make a change, gather data, figure out what is going on, and then make the change. We like the PDSA model because it formalizes that informal process and ensures that you don't skip any steps. By formalizing the process, everyone has an understanding of what will happen next. It's a useful model even when you are pursuing your own personal and career goals—you don't have to wait for greater organizational responsibility to start using it. However, as you move higher in an organization and gain more complex responsibilities, the PDSA process also becomes more complex. As a strategic leader, you put great emphasis on the planning part. It's equally important that you study and learn from what you do so that you can act in the spirit of continuous improvement. We're going to spend the rest of this chapter talking about the planning component of the PDSA model. Factor 5: Execute your strategic plan is the "do" component, and Factor 6: Make decisions to win comprise the "study" and "act" components.

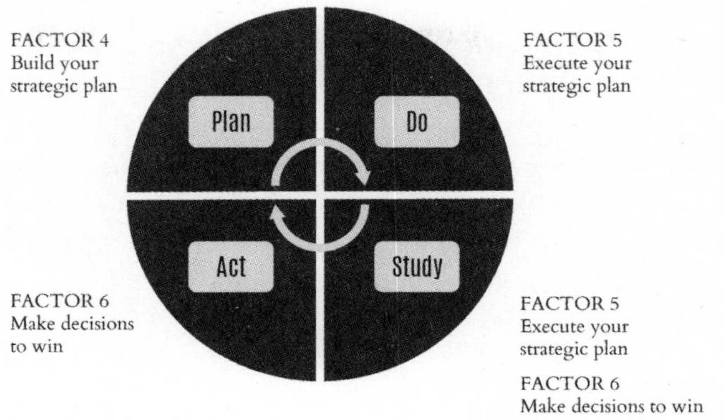

Figure 7.4

Ask the Right Business Impact Questions

Smart decisions and desired outcomes are entirely dependent upon strong planning. Albert Einstein was once asked how he would spend his time if he were given a problem upon which his life depended and he had only one hour to solve it. He responded by saying that he would spend fifty-five minutes defining the problem and five minutes solving it.[20] Strategic leaders understand the importance of planning and thinking through the problem before jumping into action. This is how they are able to make smart, informed decisions.

You don't fire, aim, ready—you ready, aim, fire!

Poorly planned projects almost always deliver confusing results, wasted time and money, uninformed decisions, and ineffective or counterproductive change. By having a plan, you have focus and structure. That doesn't mean that you aren't flexible when situations arise, but it does mean you home in on what's important and don't allow yourself to be distracted by things that aren't aligned to your goals. Many leaders have been conditioned to jump, and that can be a good trait. But you need to make sure you're jumping in the right place. You don't *fire, aim, ready*—you *ready, aim, fire*!

20 https://quoteinvestigator.com/2014/05/22/solve/

Stacey

Sometimes when I ask my clients why they made an investment in a certain program or what they expected to get out of that investment, they aren't clear and they have vague, unrealistic expectations of the desired outcome. They may have been sold something they really don't need. When this happens, I walk them through an orderly thought process to tie the investment to a corporate goal.

Remember: Purpose dominates analysis.

If you don't know where to start with your planning, business impact questions help you dig into your role in an organized fashion. When we talk about business impact questions, we are really keeping the end in mind by thinking about answers: what information does the business need to continually win? The questions must be focused to meet the needs of stakeholders and dictate the scope of your efforts. Focus is essential when you go wading into the sea of information. Once you understand what is critical to know, you can select the appropriate method for finding the answers—otherwise you become overwhelmed by data.

When we say business impact questions, we mean those questions designed to demonstrate the value of the function as a whole, such as "Are we delivering on our promise to our clients?" or "Are we delivering the value expected?" Like your functional strategy, the business questions are closely aligned to the corporate goals.

Remember: Purpose dominates analysis, or the *why* dominates the *how* when it comes to answering your business impact questions later. That means that a tool, available data, cutting-edge analytics, or a stakeholder's opinion doesn't dictate the type of analysis you conduct. Don't allow available metrics, data, software, or vendors to dictate your business impact questions. Your business impact questions dictate these things. Ask the important questions, and later you will determine how to answer them. Put the *why* and *what* before the *how*. When you're crafting business impact questions, you're building a framework. You'll come back later and figure out how to hit that target, access the necessary data to see if you're on track, and perform the right type of analysis to answer your business impact questions.

Business impact questions emerge from strategy

Recall the corporate goals for the baby store in chapter 5. One of those was

> Staff our locations with knowledgeable and friendly retail associates who will be every new parent's best friend.

We're going to walk you through an example of how Sam, as a strategic leader of the baby store's learning department, would go about drafting her business impact questions to demonstrate that her department is helping achieve a corporate goal. Sam could invite people from her team, her governance board, other stakeholders, and other organizational leaders to work with her on the planning process. She would decide who has the broadest perspective on the jungle.

During a collaborative meeting, Sam could ask:

> How do we show we are staffing our locations with knowledgeable and friendly retail associates who will be every new parent's best friend?

It would be difficult to answer this question because it is very high-level, complex, and not clearly defined. What do knowledgeable, friendly, and trusted retail associates mean to Sam's business? And as the leader of the learning department, what is Sam's role in staffing the locations? The team may decide that since Sam's department doesn't have a role in staffing the stores, they aren't directly responsible for that piece. But Sam's team is responsible for ensuring that the stores have retail associates who are knowledgeable, friendly, and trusted advisors in all locations. Here are Sam's more detailed business questions:

- Are we providing training that equips retail associates with ample product knowledge?

- Do our programs encourage associates to be friendly to customers and emphasize the importance of being friendly?
- Are we equipping associates with the knowledge and skills they need to be trusted advisors?

Now, Sam has the business impact questions she and her team need to focus on for the year. Sam knows they are the right business impact questions because they are aligned to the corporate strategy. The next steps for Sam will be to:

- Determine the impact her role needs to make on the business
- Plan *how* her team will impact the business

When using the PDSA model, it's important to remember that your business impact questions can always be refined and updated as your insights evolve. Ask yourself whether every question you plan to answer supports the vision and strategy. Strategy is like a box around what you're doing. Even unplanned business impact questions need to fit into the strategy. When finalizing business impact questions, keep track of the questions you don't ask, as well as the rationale for setting them aside. You may need to come back to them later. The questions that do make the list are the questions you will be accountable for answering, and they also need to show how your function impacts the business. Be sure they reflect what you want to show and can reasonably accomplish.

Know Your Enablers and Barriers

When drafting your business impact questions, you have to think about what you realistically can and cannot do to impact the business. At this point, you may not know what specific tasks or projects you are actually going to take on, but you need to know what is doable. In order to figure that out, make an assessment of your enablers and barriers. Enablers are the components that empower your function to do its job: the people, staff capabilities, budget, technology, political culture, environment, analytical capabilities, and more. Enablers are also the firepower you have to answer business impact questions, or the vines in the jungle that you can swing from. Barriers are the roadblocks that inhibit your function from doing its job, or the vines in the jungle that trip you up.

How you create your inventory of enablers and barriers is going to depend on the size and structure of your organization. In a more complex organization, creating your inventory may involve working with your own staff and leaders of other departments. Some organizations are so large and siloed that you may not be aware of what other departments have, or whether you can even access resources in other disciplines. In that case, you might need to rely on your stakeholders or on colleagues in other departments or functions to help you understand what already exists that you can leverage. Working with others may reveal a secret weapon or a landmine. Budget is nearly always what people think of as the top enabler or barrier, but it's not the only one. Even if your budget is tight, you can find ways to start exploring what your investments are accomplishing for the company. This is where you and your team leverage your creative and innovative abilities. Doing so will generate positive momentum for your efforts. When you are aligned with the business and able to show the impact of investments, you may find it easier to procure additional funding for investments in the future.

These are the broad categories to consider as you inventory your enablers and potential barriers; yours will vary depending on your function and industry:

Enablers (what we need and have)	**Barriers** (what we need and don't have or could derail us)
Enough budget	No or limited budget
The right people	Not enough or the wrong people
The right skillsets	Weak or the wrong skillsets/missing skillsets
Analytical/measurement capability	No or limited ability to track progress
The right technology/software	Limited or poor access to tools
Access to consulting partners	No identified or access to partners for support
Clear access to organizational data	No or limited access to broader organizational data
Political support	Political obstacles
Easy access to broader organizational knowledge/intelligence	No or limited access to organizational knowledge/intelligence

Figure 7.5

Involving your stakeholders as you inventory your enablers will ensure that your stakeholders are aware of the enablers and barriers, even more so than sharing what you've documented on your own. It's important for your stakeholders to have a realistic sense of what you can and cannot do; they may be in a position to enhance your enablers or break down barriers. If a stakeholder is pushing for something new and complex, she should be able to look at the enablers and see that you don't have the resources you need to accomplish it. Then the stakeholder can back off from the request, or—if it's important enough—help you to get what you need.

We can't answer that

Many leaders get tripped up because they start thinking about how they are going to answer the questions before even asking them. Or to put it another way, they let their current knowledge and limited access to data dictate their business impact questions. When you jump into the process of crafting your planned business impact questions, it will be tempting to shelve questions that seem too hard to answer. You may hear things like, "Don't include that question.

We can't possibly answer it." Or, "It's impossible to track that." Set those concerns aside while you brainstorm the questions, but eventually probe into the reasons behind them. Maybe you thought the data point was important, but it's actually not. Or maybe there need to be new measurements put into place. If a data point or metric is critical to achieving your goals, then you find a way. By having a functional strategy that's aligned with corporate strategy, you have a built-in business case for requesting new measurements. If resources are limited and you can't answer your business question, show them how it all fits together and help them see why you need a certain data point or metric.

This comes back to our earlier discussion about communication. Here's how Taylor and Sam approached the need for a new way of collecting data in the baby store example:

> **Taylor**
> We should put iPads in all the stores so we can track what customers are looking for! Then we'll know what time of day, week, and month their needs peak for various products. They come in, they enter their username and password into the iPad at a customer kiosk, and then they type in the product they want. By logging in, they give us the ability to track their searches, and we can link that with their customer loyalty card data via email to get a better understanding of supply chain needs.
>
> **Sam**
> Our stores are being slammed in online reviews for being out of crucial products when customers need them. Employees offer to order the product online, but customers who are coming into the store want their products right then and there. Without understanding which products are in high demand at specific points in the day, week, and month, our stores are being caught flat-footed, but they're hesitant to over-order products when they aren't sure they'll sell within a reasonable time period. The biggest hurdle here is that we aren't tracking instances where customers come into the store looking for a specific product and leave without the item they came for. If

> we can start to see the trends in these inventory holes, I would expect to see foot traffic, customer satisfaction, and same-store sales improve.

Taylor jumps right into offering a solution, which at first glance seems like a good approach. Leaders should be solution-oriented, right? The problem with Taylor's proposal is that she hasn't explained the need—she's jumped straight into collecting data. Further, her solution sounds great from the data-collection side, but pretty annoying from a customer side. Not many people enjoy being forced to log in when entering a brick-and-mortar retail store! Sam has zoomed out to the problem through big-picture thinking—customers' needs aren't being met. Did you notice her headline? We're being slammed in online reviews—ouch! With that one data point, she has the ear of any executive. Now she can propose a solution. Notice how she doesn't overwhelm her audience with the details of that solution. While she has their attention, she quickly segues into the potential benefits—improved foot traffic, customer satisfaction, and sales. If leadership wants to know the details of her plan for tracking the new data point, she can give those details in a way that's more likely to engage her audience.

People support what they help to create

Another concern when crafting business impact questions is that you may receive pushback from the team members who know they'll be responsible for the execution. They're thinking, "I have no idea how I'm going to accomplish this." Again, understand why it's important, build your business case, and then be willing to start small or negotiate. These kinds of situations get smoother when you have been planning strategically and showing impact on the business regularly over time. When leaders see what you can do with additional resources and data, they tend to get excited and want to see more. In the end, people support what they help to create.

Finalize Your Business Impact Questions

After you generate your list of initial business impact questions, refine and prioritize your list in light of your enablers and barriers. Keep in mind that you and your team will be accountable for demonstrating business impact.

- Which business concerns are most pressing or critical?
- Do you need to navigate a political situation with your stakeholders as you prioritize?
- Who among your audience most needs the insights you can provide?
- Is there a sense of urgency to answer any question first?
- Is there something about your investments that is not being answered adequately elsewhere?
- How will the resulting insights contribute to new institutional information and knowledge? Remember to think about the big picture.
- How will you overcome any barriers?
- Do you have the resources (enablers) available internally to answer the selected questions adequately?
- Do you have enough time to answer the selected question adequately?

Quick and Dirty Takeaways from This Chapter

- **Strategic planning aligns your function to the business.** Establish a strategic planning process that yields functional goals in support of applicable corporate goals.
- **Plan, Do, Study, Act.** Follow this process over and over to ensure you have a strong grasp of why you're doing what you're doing. Once it's done, look at what happened and determine if there's anything you need to change or do differently.
- **Business impact questions provide the why**. They grow out of a strong strategy that is well aligned to corporate strategy.
- **Enablers are the firepower that allow your function to do its job.** Take an inventory of what you have today, and then figure out what else you need to become a winning organization.
- **Ask the questions, and then think about how to answer them.** Don't get too hung up on your perceived lack of data or enablers. If a question is important enough to your stakeholders, you will collectively figure out how to answer it.

Chapter 8

Create Your Impact Blueprint

If you've read this book from the beginning, you aren't making changes without understanding how they contribute to business goals. You realize you can't start pulling reports, building dashboards, and investing in analytical tools without understanding what you need to learn and why you need to know it. As a strategic leader you will make decisions that may involve:

- Selecting targets of future investments
- Assessing the effectiveness of current investments
- Determining whether to discontinue existing initiatives
- Planning staffing and resource needs for the coming year
- Selling the benefits of a change to other business units

Perhaps you are doing many of these things without a formal plan or even using an ounce of quantitative data. That might be perfectly fine for the current state of your organization, but you want to be a strategic leader, which includes employing a variety of data. Using the right data can improve the outcomes of your decisions, and that data often comes in the form of business measures. Business measures are quantitative metrics (e.g., counts, percentages, time, dollars, and other financial measures) used for measurement, comparison, or to track performance or production. The values you see in your company's annual report, profit and loss statements, scorecards, or dashboards are typically business measures. Nonprofits and the government will report things like financial investments, impact values, and/or social responsibility values. These business measures are used to monitor and evaluate current business performance to make all kinds of decisions about where to invest, where to invest more, where to invest less, and where to divest in all aspects of the business.

Here's a simple example of how to act on information obtained from data. A small consultancy decides they want to start charging for the fact-finding part of the sales process. Instead of preparing sales proposals that give the client an understanding of the solution and associated price, they start pitching an up-front needs analysis with a flat cost. After sending out ten of these proposals, the sales team hasn't closed a single deal. As their pipeline drops, they decide to go back to the previous way of doing things. In this example, you don't need to run a complex data analysis—a change was made, deals stopped closing, and it's clear what the sales team should do to fix their pipeline. The way forward is obvious.

But what if you're in a function where your activities are less clearly linked to business measures, or what you do takes a long time to show up in business results? How do you know that what you're doing is working, that you're building toward success along the way? Most of us can't point to ten clearly failed proposals to say that a change was a bad decision. This is why we need to clearly establish the measures for success, and then determine the indicators that will let us know whether we're making progress toward the end goal.

Once you have generated a list of business impact questions, you continue planning by:

- Determining where you can impact business performance by pursuing your functional goals. What information do you need to answer your business impact questions?
- Deciding what investments and initiatives you need to undertake to impact the business performance. What do you need to do to make a change?

If you are in a large organization, thinking about the ways your activities affect broader business performance can be confusing and overwhelming. Even if you're in a smaller organization, it might not be straightforward—especially if you never really thought about the big picture of the business as a whole. Even if you're in charge of a part of the business, remember that all parts must work together to make the whole system work. You need to be sure your part is greased and working smoothly. You need a way to keep an eye on how your function is contributing to the big picture so that you can continuously monitor whether you are doing the right things. We recommend building an Impact Blueprint.

An Impact Blueprint is a graphical tool you can use to monitor and evaluate the performance of your function and its contributions to the business, as well as strategically plan future investments. The process of creating the Blueprint forces you to think through the impact of your current investments, and it also supports you as you plan future investments. In your Impact Blueprint, you show the link between investments and desired business outcomes. Whenever possible, build your Impact Blueprint collaboratively, especially if you have acquired a new function or department. Collaboration brings your team along with you on the journey and fosters accountability by helping them see the impact of their work. Because it's the next step from drafting business impact questions, you may choose to involve the same group of collaborators; just like the business impact questions, don't create your Blueprint in a vacuum. We have worked with many organizations to build out similar impact and measurement plans, and we've learned how critical it is to have buy-in and stakeholder accountability at the outset.

Why should you build an Impact Blueprint? Both the process and the finished product help you to:

- Think strategically about everything you do
- Demonstrate your focus on the big picture
- Foster collaboration with your team and the rest of the organization
- Demonstrate transparency to your function and stakeholders
- Embed accountability in your function
- Remove some of the complexity and confusion around selecting performance measures
- Plan evaluation and measurement activities
- See how your team's activities contribute to the business
- See where your team's activities fall short of contributing to the business

- Show your stakeholders where they can provide more direct support and remove barriers
- Make smart decisions based on data
- Build stakeholder buy-in into existing and future investments
- Communicate clearly via a visual tool
- Drive continuous improvement
- Clearly show the value of your function to the organization

The Impact Blueprint framework is similar to the logic model framework evaluators use in the nonprofit and government sectors. Once you understand how to use an Impact Blueprint, you will see just how flexible the process is, as well as the beauty of having a visual to aid communication efforts.

There are two primary scenarios for the Impact Blueprint:

1. **Scenario 1**: Assess existing Investments
   You want to build a Blueprint for investments you have already made by linking the business impact of current investments and the corporate goals.

2. **Scenario 2**: Investment Planning
   You are in the planning phase and want to make smart, informed decisions about future investments that link to corporate goals. You may be starting a new department or company, or perhaps you have used the Blueprint as a tool in Scenario 1 and are now moving forward to plan new investments.

The Impact Blueprint is equally powerful in both situations. It will help you think more strategically and help you make smarter decisions because you will have an internal process for mapping concepts, ideas, investments, and projects to corporate goals and vice versa.

These are the types of decisions you may want to make concerning a business investment:

Current Investment

- Do we continue an investment?
- Do we stop an investment?
- Do we modify an investment?
- Do we reinvest elsewhere?
- How do we optimize our investment?

Investment Planning

- Do we invest?
- In what should we invest?
- How do we optimize our investment?

Now, let's build some Blueprints to help make it clear and answer our sample business impact questions.

Existing investments

When you have known initiatives or investments, you start by building out the frame of your Impact Blueprint.

Part 1: The functional goals & business impact questions

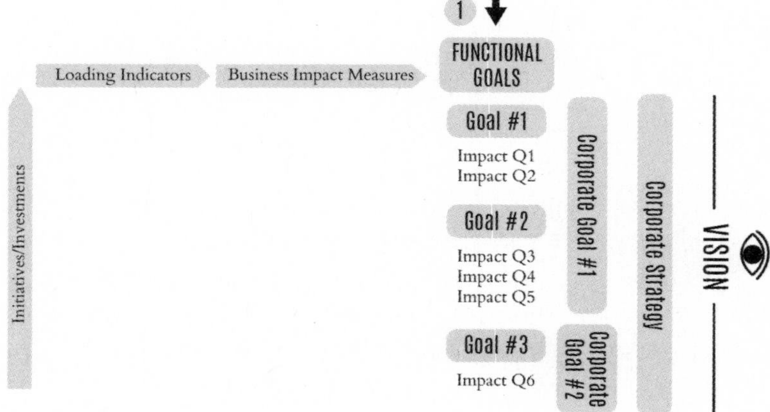

Figure 8.1

We begin with the end in mind. First, you list the strategic organizational goals aligned to your functional goals on the right. Under each goal, list the business impact questions you generated for each goal.

If you don't have a functional strategy that is tightly aligned to corporate strategy and vision (or don't know how to develop one), we strongly urge you to go back and read chapter 5 before you attempt to create an Impact Blueprint. The corporate strategy, extending into your functional strategy, will dictate all of your decisions. When your strategy is clear and well-aligned to corporate's, your decisions become clear in turn.

Part 2: The investments

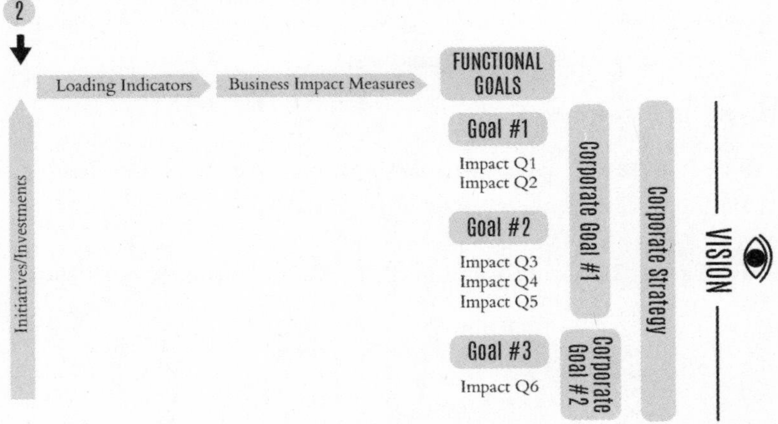

Figure 8.2

Now we jump over to the far left section of the Impact Blueprint. What are the initiatives, programs, projects, investments, and activities that your department or function is taking on? You don't necessarily have to list out all of your projects and activities, but you should include the significant or most important initiatives/investments.

Now, you have the frame of your Impact Blueprint built. The next step is to link your existing investments to your functional strategy by documenting your assumptions or theory of how you think your investments will impact business performance.

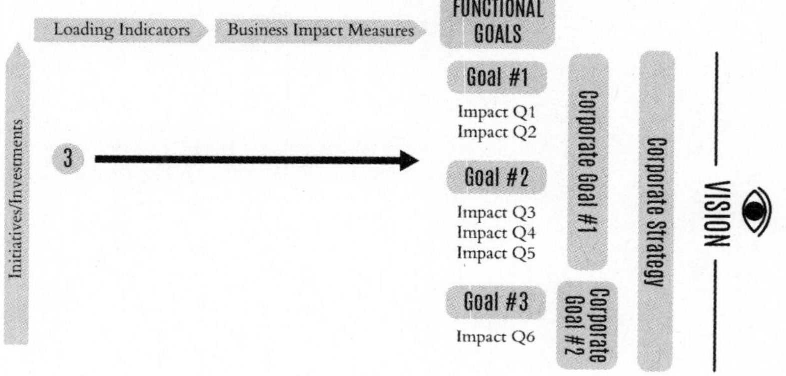

Figure 8.3

The Impact Blueprint allows you to identify the direct, indirect, or even nonexistent links between your initiatives/investments and your functional strategy. If your initiatives are complex, you may want to build an Impact Blueprint for each one or make Blueprints for different categories of investments (such as people, products, projects, etc.). Sometimes you won't know if you want multiple Impact Blueprints until you start building one and uncover the need to break it out to simplify your thinking and ease communication.

Part 3: Leading indicators of business impact and Measures of business impact

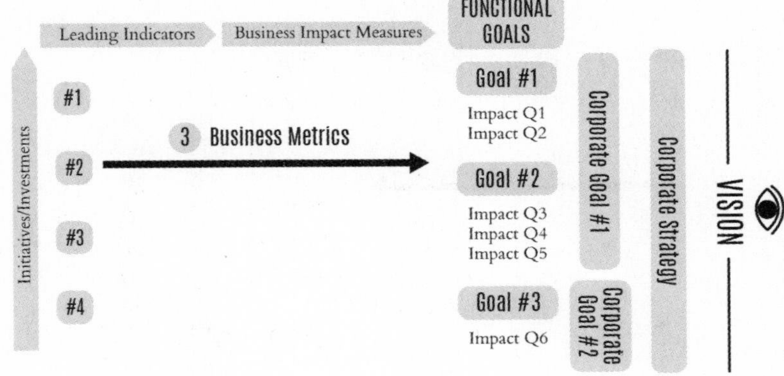

Figure 8.4

As you start thinking through your assumptions of how your investments impact your strategy, you start by asking if/then questions. That is, if you invested in project X, then you expect that business metric Y will change. In most cases, an investment will impact multiple business measures. To figure out how those measures are linked to the corporate strategy, you map them on the Impact Blueprint under either leading indicators of business impact or measures of business impact.

For the Impact Blueprint, we classify a business metric as a leading indicator of business impact if it indicates or leads to a later measure of business impact. You may have heard the term leading indicators in the past—these signal a future event or activity, indicating that business impact could happen. Leading indicators of business impact are usually a basic count or status, such as the number of customers served, the number of training courses completed, the number of sales calls made, the average time to complete a project, the number of houses sold, time to problem resolution, number of hot meals served, etc. These metrics all indicate something could happen in the future, but they don't clearly show business impact on their own. You are doing something and have a lot of activity going on, but are your activities making an impact on the business? Remember, it's irrelevant how many trees the producers cut down if they aren't in the right jungle.

While leading indicators of business impact tell you if you're on track to reach the goals on the right side, a measure of business impact is typically a lagging indicator because it follows an event. Measures of business impact are usually financial, such as revenue generated, operating margin, cost savings, etc. If they aren't financial, they are things for which the business knows the dollar value—for example, each 5 percent decrease in employee turnover represents a fixed cost savings.

You may see the results of some of your leading indicators of business impact or measures of business impact quickly, some in a few weeks or months, and some in a year or even multiple years. In any case, you can map them as short-, mid- or long-term metrics. In the end, it's up to you how you map your impact, as long as you have established clear differences between the leading indicators of business impact and the measures of business impact. The activity of the workers on the jungle floor can be measured in a number of ways, like sharpness of the machetes, brawn of the cutters, number of trees felled per hour, etc. Remember, though, that these activities need to be performed in the right jungle to be meaningful. The measure of business impact might be something like total sales of cleared jungle land to farmers who plan to turn it into farmland. That's where the workers are impacting the business in a meaningful way. If their leading indicators are strong but they aren't being performed in the right jungle, none of that activity ends up mattering. What if you've cleared the land in the wrong jungle and no farmer wants to buy it? The land will lie fallow. That, in a nutshell, is the danger of making major decisions based on leading indicators alone.

Let's use a simplified example to illustrate how to build an Impact Blueprint for a planned initiative or investment.

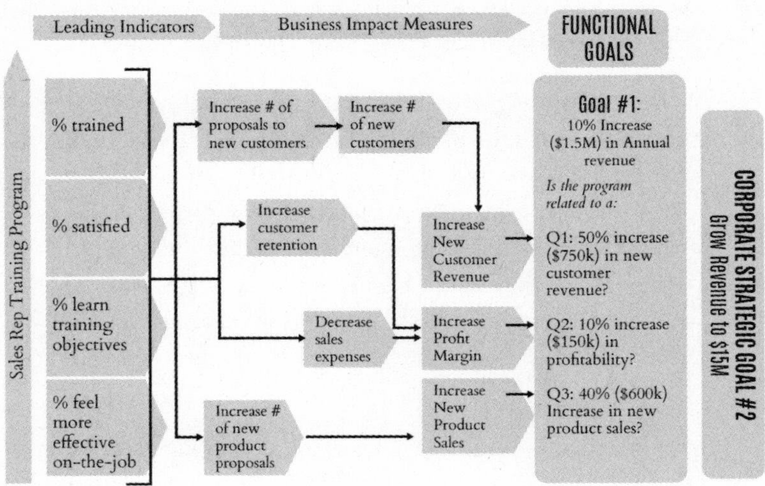

Figure 8.5

Say you have made an investment in a sales rep training program to improve the skills and knowledge of the sales force. You made this training investment to achieve a functional goal of increasing revenue by 15 percent in an effort to contribute to hitting a corporate goal to grow revenue to $15 million. Following the sales rep training, you may know the figures for:

- Percentage of sales representatives trained
- Percentage of sales representatives satisfied with the training program
- Percentage of sales representatives who reported that they learned the objectives of the training program
- Percentage of sales representatives who reported they are now more efficient on the job

These are all indicators that your training program impacted the corporate goal of increasing revenue by 15 percent, but they don't directly link your training program to the goal. Technically, these would be considered vanity metrics, because they show that you did something and they look good, but did you do the right thing? So the next question is, how have the trained sales representatives performed in the field after the training? Was there:

- An increase in the number of new customers they brought in?
- An increase in overall customer satisfaction?
- A decrease in sales expenses?
- An increase in the number of new product proposals?

If your program was designed to impact these business metrics, did it? These are leading indicators, because they don't directly increase sales revenue. All of these metrics are your theory of how the training program changes the sales force. We theorize that the sales representatives changed the way they did their jobs after training, but did they in turn change the business? You have to take your questioning to the next level and ask:

- Now that we have an increase in the number of new customers, how much revenue did we receive from them?
- Now that we had an increase in customer satisfaction, how much additional revenue did we receive from our current customers?
- Now that we have reduced sales expenses, did we see an increase in profit margin?
- Now that we have an increase in the number of new product proposals, did we sell more of the new products?

All of these metrics are business impact metrics: sales expenses, net revenue, profit margin and new product sales. We put these in the business metrics category because they have a financial value and are directly linked to our goal of increasing revenue. The only exception here is the sales expenses—a decrease in sales expenses is a financial measure that indicates an increase in profit margin. Thus, our theory is that if training the sales force moves the needle on these leading indicators, then that should influence the business metrics, which in turn impact the goal of increasing revenue. Assessing the impact of your investments is living the culture of accountability, and the Impact Blueprint helps you to do it transparently.

Investment planning

As a leader, it's your responsibility to be a good steward of your budget, using it in the most efficient way possible to achieve organizational goals. The Impact Blueprint can clarify how you're going to use your budget and highlight when an investment may not be the best choice for the corporate goal.

When planning for investments, you build your Impact Blueprint from the right (goals) to the left (investments).

You start with the first goal and ask what changes you need to make to achieve that goal. What would you expect to happen as a result of your proposed changes? In our previous example, the functional goal was to increase revenue by 15 percent.

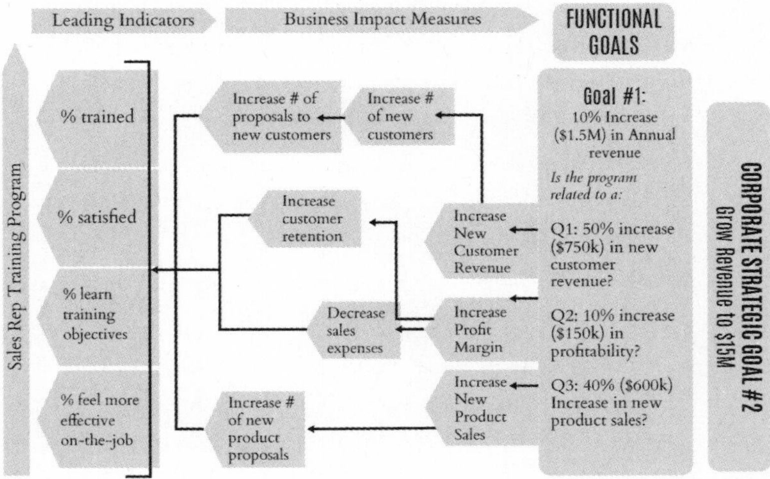

Figure 8.6

If we want to increase revenue by 15 percent, what do we need to do? What would we expect to see as a result? We'd need:

- Revenue from new customers
- More new revenue from existing customers
- Increased profit margin
- Increased sales of new products

Then you ask how you would accomplish each goal:

- How will we get revenue from new customers? By reaching out to new potential targets and offering products and services that match their needs.
- How will we get more revenue from existing customers? By increasing current customer satisfaction.
- How will we increase profit margin? By decreasing our sales expenses.
- How will we increase sales of our new product? By putting out more sales proposals that include the new product.

How do we accomplish those goals? We need to train the sales representatives in the above areas. Maybe you instinctively knew you needed sales training, or you had a stakeholder asking for it. By going through this exercise of creating the Impact Blueprint, you have taken a systematic approach to deciding whether the sales training program is the right investment to impact the business, in a way that embeds the design of an evaluation plan wherein everybody understands the measures of success. Because you build your Blueprint collaboratively, you are also doing so with knowledge of your unique business needs. Maybe there is a customer dissatisfaction problem that can't be solved with sales training—if you're making your Blueprint in a vacuum, you may not be aware of that circumstance, and although your Blueprint will look great, it won't actually lead to a win.

This is a simple example to illustrate the construction process. In reality, your Blueprint may be much more detailed and complex. However, to use the Blueprint as a strategic tool, you should keep it as simple as possible and may even need a simplified, rolled-up version for executive communication purposes. We invite you to download an Impact Blueprint template from our site at www.bemorestrategicinbusiness.com.

Remember, we are still in the planning part of our PDSA model. As you create the Blueprint, you aren't yet determining *how* you'll measure these leading indicators or business impact metrics, who will capture the data, when you will do it, etc. The Impact Blueprint framework isn't about the *how*, and focusing there will stall your process. Focus on the change you want to see, or the *what*, considered in light of the *why*. After going through the process of fine-tuning and iterating your Impact Blueprint, you settle on your final metrics. Then you can discuss *how* you will execute the process of collecting those metrics, and in the case of an investment-planning Blueprint, *how* to deploy the investments. If you've worked collaboratively, your stakeholders will ideally help you get the metrics you need, too.

Use the language of your organization

There are business metrics for each of your company's functions: sales, marketing, human resources, IT, each of the operations departments, the project management office, learning and development, etc. Do you know what business metrics or success metrics are used in your own department? If there aren't any, then you have identified a strategic gap. Each function monitors and tracks their performance across time. You may have a person or entire strategic function that is responsible for evaluating the strategic performance of your departments individually and across the business as a whole. If so, find and befriend these people. They will be great assets to you as a strategic leader. Consider inviting them to help build your Impact Blueprint, because they can see across the entire jungle. Many of the functional metrics (at the department level) roll up into financial metrics (finance office), and that's because, from a big-picture perspective, some of the functional metrics are leading indicators that indicate business impact.

Important note! When it's time to select the business metrics for your Impact Blueprint, you may find that people call business metrics different things in your organization. Ideally, businesses should have clear terms and language for measuring business performance, but that may not be your reality. You may hear things such as key performance indicators (KPIs), critical success measures, leading and lagging indicators, outcomes, metrics, business results, economic indicators, or social results. Each function and each person may have a different name. Overall, these are measures of how the various functions conduct their respective business, and at some point the measures are all rolled up to gauge the overall performance of the business. As a strategic leader, you should either follow the standard for business metrics your business dictates, if they have one, or create and model a standard within your function. If you use the Impact Blueprint for strategic planning, then you can use the terms *leading indicators* and *business impact measures* to classify your functional metrics. You can also reclassify your Impact Blueprint metrics to best align to your organization. If you use leading and lagging indicators, change business impact measures to lagging indicators. The Impact Blueprint is a tool to help you with strategic planning. Customize it to work for your business.

When you are making your assumptions and mapping your business metrics across your Blueprint, you will find that some business impact metrics will change much sooner than others. For instance, you may have sales results each business quarter, and then an annual sales number. The quarterly sales results are short-term business impact metrics, while the annual sales number may be considered a mid- or long-term business impact metric. You can lay out your impact metrics by short-, mid-, and long-term.

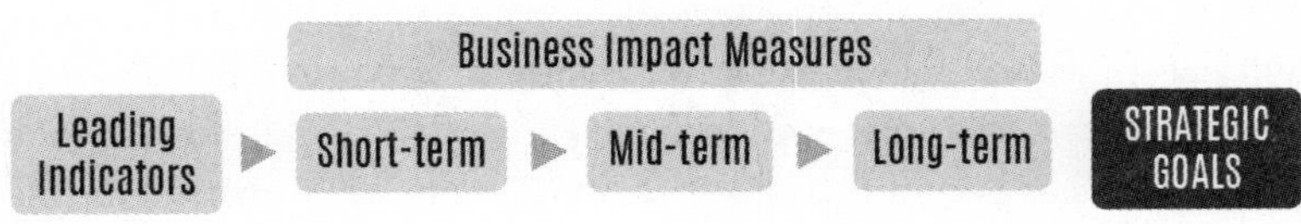

Figure 8.7

As a reminder, business metrics on your Impact Blueprint will be quantitative, not qualitative. That means they will be reported with a number. It may be a number that reflects qualitative data (e.g., number of customer positive comments, number of customer complaints, percent of employees satisfied with the new HR program, etc.). Most of your qualitative (non-numerical) data usually comes from people (employees, customers, leaders, influencers, industry experts, etc.) via surveys, focus groups, interviews, and/or benchmarking activities. You have to convert or summarize your qualitative data to quantitative data to see patterns and trends. This converted number is what you use on your Impact Blueprint.

Strategic planning is based on informed assumptions of what will happen in the business, industry, country, and/or world during a certain timeframe (one-year or multi-year). These assumptions are rooted in peoples' business experience, existing organizational intelligence, hard evidence from internal and external data, known industry patterns and trends, forecasts, predictions, gut feel, or some combination of all the above. At some point, every decision has to start with assumptions (or theories) because there is insufficient evidence to claim it as a fact. Every day businesses make people, products, tools, technology, and/or program investments based on assumptions that the investment will make some business impact and provide a return.

For instance, when a company makes a new hire, they are making assumptions based on that person's past performance that they will get a return on their investment in that person. They have to assume that based on the knowledge and data they have about that person (i.e., resume, interview perceptions and ratings, any networking feedback, recruiter notes, social media presence, portfolio or knowledge of previous work outcomes, assessment of cultural fit, personality/leadership assessment, drug test results, etc.), the business will get some payback. Some new hire assumptions end up proving to be excellent decisions once you have more hard evidence of work performance, while some result in a loss. The bottom line is that the business had to start somewhere, and they started with assumptions based on the best data they had about that person.

So no matter what function or department you are in, strategic planning is critical. Yes, your Impact Blueprint may start with some informed and some uninformed assumptions or theories about how a certain initiative or investment will impact the business, but as you monitor your investments and gather more data over time, you build more evidence to update and refine your assumptions (i.e., continuous improvement); then you start moving from assumptions to hard evidence and get closer to facts.

Your Impact Blueprint can be used in many ways:

1. **Gain stakeholder buy-in.** Show your stakeholders a visual blueprint of your planned business impact. A visual will reduce or eliminate miscommunication. The blueprint highlights exactly where you expect to see impact. In the end, as the leader, you are the one who has to defend it, so take a consultative approach to incorporating any feedback.

2. **Foster collaboration with your team and the rest of the organization.** Simply the process of collaborating on a map of your functional strategy goes a long way toward relationship building and demonstrating transparency.

3. **Embed accountability into your function.** You can use the Blueprint to visualize and communicate the business impact across the organization. The Blueprint is your dashboard or scorecard that holds you and your team accountable for business results. For instance, you can highlight or change the colors of Blueprint metrics that were or were not impacted by the investment. Keep it updated as time goes on.

4. **Remove some of the complexity and confusion around selecting business performance measures.** The Blueprint framework and your business impact questions create structure around the business impact you need to demonstrate. That structure allows you to focus on a precise set of business impact questions, and you only need the metrics that will answer those questions.

5. **Plan evaluation and measurement activities.** The Impact Blueprint serves as your execution plan to answer your business impact questions. A simplified planning process will eliminate confusion and help you get the most out of the time and resources you spend demonstrating the value of your function.

6. **See how your team's activities contribute to the business and where you fall short.** As you lead your team through your jungle, you have a map to guide you and redirect you as needed. When you get off track, you can come back to the Blueprint to see what you must accomplish and make adjustments as needed.

7. **Make smart decisions based on data.** As a strategic leader, you can make decisions based on hard data.

8. **Drive continuous improvement.** Since you will continually update your Blueprint, you will continually add value to the organization. You'll also be able to see areas for improvement along the way.

9. **Blue-sky Impact Blueprint.** You can create two Impact Blueprints. One can be a blue-sky plan that may include unavailable metrics or analyses that cannot be executed at this time due to limited enabling factors. The benefit of the blue-sky Impact Blueprint is that stakeholders will know what you need to get there, and they may be able to close those gaps for you.

10. **Tie existing investments to corporate goals.** Everybody has to start somewhere, and chances are you'll create your first Blueprint for an existing investment that isn't clearly impacting the business. If you can't transparently align the investment to the corporate goals, it should trigger you to make a decision about that investment. You may need to make an immediate change.

Regardless of whether you've created your Blueprint in the process of planning investments or are using the Blueprint to figure out how existing activities align to strategy, you now have a clear map of your jungle. In reality, no map is perfect, and no map is ever complete. There are detours, rock slides, construction, floods that create unexpected bodies of water—maps need to evolve over time, and travelers need to pay close attention to their surroundings. If you create your Impact Blueprint and then just put your head down and follow through on the planned investments, you will neglect the changes occurring around you all the time. Your Blueprint gives you a foundation for making smart decisions, but there's more work to do.

Quick and Dirty Takeaways from This Chapter

- **Start with business impact questions.** When you sit down to build your Impact Blueprint, think about what you need to know. What information will help you make decisions in the short-, medium-, and long-term?
- **Use the Impact Blueprint as a tool.** Ideally a Blueprint will guide your planning, but in reality, that's not always the case. It can also help you figure out the alignment and success metrics for investments already in place. Make it a useful tool for your particular situation!
- **Understand the difference between leading indicators of business impact and measures of business impact.** Are you in the right jungle? How do you know you are making progress toward your goal?

Checklist for Factor 4: Build your strategic plan

- ☐ Are you following the Plan, Do, Study, Act model?
- ☐ Do you have a list of business impact questions that will provide what you need to know in order to continuously win?
- ☐ Have you created an inventory of your enablers?
- ☐ Have you created an Impact Blueprint that is vetted and supported by your stakeholders?
- ☐ Are you using leading indicators of business impact and business impact measures appropriately, making decisions within the context of the right jungle?

Figure 8.8

Chapter 9

Factor 5—Execute Your Strategic Plan

The last two chapters went into great detail about planning because a strong plan is an important tool for staying on track toward your goals. That said, it's easy to fall into a trap of endlessly planning and never getting anything done! At some point, you have to step back from the plan and put it into action. Smart, strategic leaders execute the projects and investments that will influence the metrics on the Impact Blueprint. By going through the process of creating the Blueprint, you've built a map to your desired destination—the business goals on the right side of the Blueprint. Executing along the Blueprint means everything you do is aligned with the outcomes you expect, and you are acting in alignment with the business instead of creating activities that you hope will move the needle on some important metric somewhere. It's at this point that real life gets thrown into the mix, and many leaders get confused. Things don't always go according to plan—how do you know what to do when the unexpected happens?

Change

When it comes to executing your plan, there are two types of change that will come into play:

- The measurable change you are driving with your actions and investments
- The uncontrollable change constantly happening in the world around you

These two types of change are often at odds. For example, you may be executing toward a certain goal, but suddenly there is a shift in the market or a major event in the world that renders your goal irrelevant or inadequate. An important part of leadership is maintaining the delicate balance between these two types of change. As much as you are staying in tune with the change driven by your work, you are also in touch with the market and world around you to make sure you don't suddenly find yourself in the wrong jungle.

Here's the danger of executing strictly according to plan: do you remember Crystal Pepsi? It was supposed to taste like Pepsi, but the color was clear instead of the traditional brown. The product was a flop in the market, leaving consumers with a highly disappointing bad taste in their mouths.[21] David Novak, who later became the CEO of Yum Brands, was the brains behind the product; he later told *Fast Company*:

> I still think it's the best idea I ever had, and the worst executed. A lot of times as a leader you think, "They don't get it; they don't see my vision." People were saying we should stop and address some issues along the way, and they were right. It would have been nice if I'd made sure the product tasted good. Once you have a great idea and you blow it, you don't get a chance to resurrect it.[22]

Novak had a plan for this product but failed to see that he ultimately ended up in the wrong jungle during the execution phase. The product went to market anyway, and Pepsi had to pull it off the shelves, losing money and suffering harm to its reputation.

Here's another example, from a consumer brand that suffered a setback and responded in kind. Tropicana decided to change the design of its orange juice cartons, and consumers were outraged. "We underestimated the deep emotional bond' loyal customers had with the original packaging, Neil Campbell, president of Tropicana North America in Chicago explained."[23] Within a month of the change, the juice was back in its original packaging. Here, Tropicana recognized the need to cut its losses on the design and switch back to what its customers wanted.

Both of these examples highlight the most common occurrence that changes your best-laid plans in the business world: customers' changing needs and desires. Whether your customers are external (buying the company's products and services) or internal (other employees or departments you service), they are your *raison d'etre*! Customers' needs are constantly changing, and one of the biggest mistakes you can make in business is to continue to execute along a

---

21 https://consumerist.com/2016/06/30/17-commercial-failures-from-brands-with-spectacularly-bad-ideas/

22 https://www.fastcompany.com/60555/winging-it

23 https://consumerist.com/2016/06/30/17-commercial-failures-from-brands-with-spectacularly-bad-ideas/

plan that no longer meets those needs. So, have a strong plan that's well-aligned to business goals, but also keep an ear to the ground and be ready to change as needed. One way the Impact Blueprint makes you a stronger leader is that it gives you a platform to return to in times of crisis. In the Tropicana example above, the package designers responded quickly when it became clear that the new juice carton wasn't a hit with customers. But what did they do once they resolved the crisis situation? Our best practice is to come back to the Impact Blueprint. The goal of satisfying customers still stands. What do you need to adjust in order to get back on track toward achieving that goal? Edit your Blueprint using the same process you used to create it:

- The goal is X.
- How do we accomplish X?
- To accomplish X, we do A.
- How do we accomplish A?
- To accomplish A, we do C.
- How do we accomplish C?
- We invest in these five areas.

Now we have theorized that investing in the stated five areas is the right thing to do because it will drive value all the way back to the goal of X. We're back on track and ready to try again.

Use the Rungs of the Ladder

Come back to the ladder we're building in the jungle. Here on the fifth rung, you're getting close to being able to see over the tops of the trees. You're still climbing up and down, working with your teams on the jungle floor as much as you are looking up. The other steps you hit along the way are critical success factors when you execute. In order to stay in touch with customer needs and understand where the marketplace is going, you can't operate in a vacuum. You need to rely on your governance board and stakeholders to help fill out your vision of what's happening around you. It's a recipe for failure to create a plan, press go, and walk away. Instead, you execute in iterations, constantly asking business impact questions and seeking the data needed to answer them. You made your plan with the best information that was available at the time. Reserve the right to get smarter as you go along, and don't be afraid to change course when you realize you're in the wrong jungle! Learning from personal and organizational failures or errors is an important aspect of being a strategic leader. Smart leaders know failure is expected and accepted from themselves, their teams, and their organization. Leaving room for mistakes isn't just about covering your butt when bad things happen. It's about giving people the space to fail, learn, and do better.

Build and Lead a Winning Team for Everyday Execution

As a strategic leader, you're at the head of a high-functioning, winning group of people who are executing on the component parts of your plan. How do you get them to row together, moving forward instead of pushing the boat around in a circle? The principles of communication in chapter 3 are critical for leading a successful team. Keeping communication open and frequent underlies all of the other pieces. Here are some other approaches to getting everyone rowing in unison.

Provide an inspirational vision

If you're building your ladder from the ground up, you already have a strong vision for your function that's aligned to the business. Make sure everyone on your team knows that vision inside and out. Talk about it constantly; what are you trying to achieve? Show your team that you can all achieve the vision together. Foster a desire to do things differently, to achieve something bigger than what feels possible or what has been done in the past. Remember, as a strategic leader, you are always communicating about the vision with your peers in leadership. You can leverage your team to help reinforce the vision, too. Do you have team members who regularly interact with executives? Groom them to think and communicate in the strategic way you are learning to do in this book. Even team members who don't often leave their desks should be able to clearly articulate how the company makes money and how their work contributes to that. Your team, from top to bottom, should all feel closely aligned to the company's mission.

Have the right people in the right roles

Recruit, hire, train, and develop team players who have the ability and passion to bring your vision to life. This is something that is relatively straightforward if you're building a team from scratch but becomes more complicated when you step into the role of leading an existing team. The fact of the matter is that if you don't have the right team members in the appropriate places, you can't achieve your vision. Ask yourself: is each team member doing work that matches his skill set, competency level, motivation, and desire? If the answer is no, why is that person in that role? Can he be more successful in another role? Does he need additional training or resources to be successful? New leaders often make the mistake of keeping a mediocre employee in a poorly fitting role for one reason or another. Unfortunately, we've learned the hard way that it's nearly impossible to win without good people. The amount of effort you will put into trying to turn that person into a winning contributor so rarely pays off. Start with people who have the right attitude toward the work, and always be on the lookout for ways you can develop their talents and provide them with opportunities for advancement.

When you're building a team, don't forget to leverage diversity. It's a well-documented truth that diversity on teams drives innovation. By the same token, leading a team of people who are just like you will be the worst team you ever run. Everyone brings the same point of view and wants to take on the same projects. There's no diversity of thought and skills.

Create a work environment where people will thrive. Celebrate success!

Your role as a leader is to remove the barriers that keep your team members from doing their jobs. Are they lacking important tools, resources, or information? Help them to fill those gaps with the necessary enablers so that they can successfully do their jobs. In the meantime, you keep everyone focused on and accountable for executing the goal at hand, and you also recognize successful milestones along the way. Athletes in almost every sport understand this: a football team doesn't wait for a touchdown to jump around and celebrate. You see the players exchanging high fives and back slaps every time they gain yards. They are keeping each other motivated by celebrating the little successes that lead to the big goal.

Foster authenticity and transparency

Authenticity requires hiring and retaining people who believe in your brand and the work you're doing. They may not agree with every decision, but they buy into the overall mission. It also comes from the top—by communicating clearly and reminding your team of the unifying vision, you keep everybody on the same page. Transparency is closely linked to authenticity, and there are many ways you can work transparently. When you build the scorecard for your function, share it regularly with your team. Use the Impact Blueprint to help them see the ways their work impacts the measures on the scorecard. Show how you go about making decisions, not only to maintain transparency, but also to help develop the decision-making abilities of the people on your team.

When your team isn't functioning

If you find yourself leading a team that isn't functioning the way it should be, consider what's happening in light of the four items above. Ask yourself:

- Is the vision clear? Is everybody on board with the vision?
- Do I have the right people on the team doing the right jobs?
- Is each team member clear about her role in bringing the vision to life? Is each person's job role clear?
- Can team members see how their roles connect to the big picture?

- Are team members accountable for their actions?
- Do I need to recognize or redirect any team members?
- Am I inspiring the team and gaining their commitment with my leadership?

Recognizing and redirecting are powerful tools for ongoing team management. Recognize and reward your team members in the ways they like to be recognized. When you want them to do something differently, find ways to redirect their actions. Inspire and gain commitment at every level.

Using Data to Show Progress on Your Impact Blueprint

Once you've created your Blueprint, you have the basic architecture to create a data analysis plan, which will enable you to show progress toward your goals. You have decided exactly what business metrics you need to track, and so you're ready to go after the necessary data. As a strategic leader, you probably will not be the one to create or execute the data analysis plan. You will hand your Blueprint over to a data analyst or consultant who will do the math-magic to answer your business impact questions. As a leader, you will have an advantage if you can speak their language, express your desired outcomes, and understand the basics of what they are saying when they consult with you.

Your goal is to answer the business impact questions following the assumptions you made—nothing more and nothing less at this point. Don't be persuaded by an over-zealous data analyst to go down any rabbit holes or investigate any potentially interesting alternatives. You need to stay focused on uncovering the answers to your questions so you have the information you need to make decisions, continuously improve, and deliver winning results. When you get into the weeds with statisticians, they may tell you that the results from their analyses do not give definite answers, but instead suggest new assumptions, theories, or decisions that are subject to further testing. This is where business diverges sharply from academics: at some point, you have to make a decision with the best information available and move on. Don't fall into the trap of analysis paralysis.

You have to decide when you have enough information to make a strategic decision. In the end, you are the one who has to stand up in front of your peers and defend the answers to your questions. Be sure you understand the answers and how they are tied to your questions—that is, are you delivering results that are meaningful to the business?

We live in a world full of data. To ignore data's ability to improve your decision-making and planning is like ignoring anything else that gives you a competitive edge in business. If you don't take the advantage, you'll quickly be left behind. We know data and analytics can be overwhelming in a unique way. There are people who spend their whole careers studying the math behind turning raw data into actionable insights for making decisions. You don't need to understand all the details behind the analytical techniques and statistics, but you need to know enough to stay on track and be sure you don't stray from the intended purpose. You can take advantage of their expertise by having a basic understanding of the concepts and tools they work with.

To simplify the world of data analytics a bit for you, we made five categories into which your business impact questions will fall that will dictate how the data can be analyzed to give you the answers you want. There are many nuisances behind each categories and more technical aspects that we don't go into here. From here you can source data analytic resources—hire, borrow from other departments, contract with a consultant, purchase software, etc. In your data analysis plan, your data analytic resource will take each business impact question, show which business metric you need to answer that question (as you put in your Blueprint), list how to collect those metrics, and what type of analysis is required to answer the question. Because you began with business impact questions, you have clear outcomes for these data analytic resources.

1. **Status**
   Actively monitor the current state of initiatives and investments.

   These descriptive metrics can give you limited insights into how the investment is performing in real time. These are typical dashboard, scorecard, and infographic metrics. Sometimes these are called descriptive or vanity metrics. Vanity metrics make an investment look good, showing a superficial level of accomplishment—for example, number of items manufactured, number of clicks on a digital ad, percent of employee with performance reviews, etc. Alone, these numbers don't mean much when it comes to the real, organizational value of the initiative. They may inform decisions, but you must be cautious making major decisions based on status metrics alone. For example, you wouldn't cancel a national advertising campaign because click-through rates are lower on the third day the campaign is running. However, you would watch closely to see if click-throughs and other metrics start to improve soon, and you would also look for other factors that may be hurting ad performance. The status of investment activities tells you if you are making progress in the right direction.

2. **Relationships**

What is the relationship between the investment and business performance?

Relationships between participation in an initiative and any one or more of the business performance metrics on your Blueprint give you an idea of whether the initiative is related to any of your desired metrics. These types of relationships are established via statistical techniques called correlation and regression. You are probably familiar with the expression "correlation doesn't equal causation." Although the factors appear to have some relationship, it doesn't mean one caused the other. There may be some other external forces you didn't account for or know to account for that significantly contributed to the relationship. For example, what is the relationship between using a new logistics provider and on-time deliveries to customers? Are the customers receiving their deliveries on time because of the provider, or is it because warmer weather has resulted in fewer road delays? Maybe we can't give the logistics provider credit for more on-time deliveries, but we can say that on-time deliveries began to increase at the same time that we started using the new provider. Of course, we would love to know if our investment *caused* business performance, but we need more data and more precision to make that leap. For monitoring purposes, you can track relationships between your investments and business performance metrics to see if they vary.

3. **Impact**
   How did the investment impact the business in the past?

   Impact analysis is one of the most robust analytical approaches you can undertake. You compare changes in one or more business impact metrics between comparable groups: one of which was exposed to the initiative or investment and another that was not exposed. If there is a difference between the two groups, you have hard evidence and a strong case that your initiative or investment impacted business performance. Remember our sales representative training Blueprint in chapter 8? We could compare performance on the Blueprint business metrics between those who participated in the training and those who did not participate. You still can't imply that your investment caused a certain movement in business performance, but you have hard evidence that it made a difference. Impact analyses requires stronger enablers—access to analytical capability like a social scientist, data analysist, data scientist, statistician, stakeholder support, software, etc. In return for these resources, impact provides more precise insights and gives you more confidence when making decisions.

4. **Predictive**
   How could the investment impact the business in the future?

   The term predictive analytics refers to the use of statistical techniques for predictive modeling; this may include machine learning and data mining to predict some future scenario based on past data. Firms often use predictive analytics to explain a phenomenon they want to understand (e.g., why did customer retention drop last month?); predict things about the future (e.g., what will sales look like over the next six months if we hire additional reps?); or to decide what to do (e.g., what will happen to gross revenue if we open a new store in Thailand next year?) Your Netflix and Amazon personalized recommendations are generated by predictive analytics. These types of predictions are based on models of existing data and the probability that something will occur. Predictive analytics provides extensive business knowledge, which yields high organizational decision-making value.

5. **Prescriptive Analytics**
   What recommendations for action can we prescribe to drive future business impact?

   Prescriptive analytics take predictive analytics to the next level. The use of prescriptive analytics is a complex statistical approach to making recommendations based on prediction models. This approach predicts what will happen, when it will happen, and why it will happen. As more and more data are fed into the predictive models, the system learns and can make smarter recommendations that minimize business risk. Prescriptive analytics give decision makers more information about the impact of options, leading to reduced business risk and faster decisions. Driverless cars are an example of a technology run on prescriptive analytics. The car system is the decision maker, and it has to make multiple decisions quickly based on predictions of future outcomes.

Let's use a simple medical example to show how all five categories can work together. *Status* metrics are the individual numbers your medical provider tracks at each appointment—height, weight, blood pressure, cholesterol, blood sugar, family history, etc. Individually, each number doesn't tell you a whole lot. Considering the *relationships* between these pieces of information begins to show the medical provider where to investigate further. An unhealthy BMI, high blood sugar, and a family history of diabetes may indicate an increased risk of the patient developing diabetes. The provider orders diabetes testing and the test comes back negative. This is analogous to the *impact*, because it shows what has happened in the past. However, all the indicators *predict* that the patient is at risk of diabetes in the future. In spite of the current negative test, that patient is still at risk, so the provider *prescribes* a low sugar diet and follow-up testing within a year.

These five categories of evaluation activities will feed into the way you answer your business impact questions. Usually a data analyst, data scientist, statistician, or evaluator takes a hard look at each question and determines which type of analysis is required to answer it. Here's a basic example of an investment's business questions mapped into each category of analysis:

> **Goal:** Build a safe IT infrastructure
>
> **Investment:** A trial program for a new cybersecurity software system
>
> **Business questions**
>
> > **Status:** Is the trial software installed on our system? Is it running 24/7? How many threats did it deflect in the last twenty-four hours?
> >
> > **Relationships:** Are we seeing fewer risks and threats now than we saw before the software was installed?
> >
> > **Impact:** Are we seeing fewer risks and threats on the trial systems than on the systems that don't have the trial software?
> >
> > **Predictive:** Can the trial software reduce risks, threats, and vulnerability if deployed systemwide?
> >
> > **Prescriptive:** What server settings and level of complexity do we need to use to gain the maximum reduction in risks and threats?

As you use more complex analytic techniques, you will need greater resources and enablers, and you also gain stronger decision-making capabilities. The chart below shows where each technique fits based on enablers and decision-making needs.

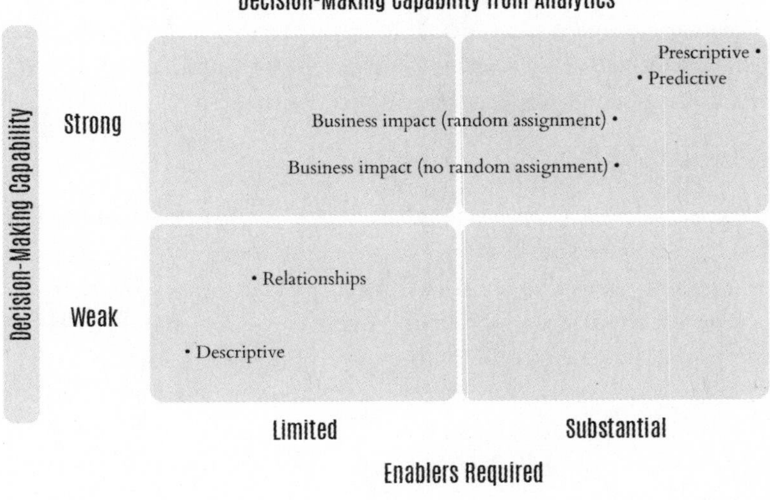

Figure 9.1

It's critical to understand that not every business question requires a predictive analysis. In a perfect world, your data analytics resource employs the strongest analytic technique available to answer the relevant questions. The strongest technique provides you with greater decision-making capability, which gives you stronger business intelligence and reduces risk. In practice, not all organizations can deploy a rigorous evaluation of investments, and not all situations warrant it. This is why it's so important to understand your business culture, build a culture of accountability with your stakeholders, and know your enablers. When creating business impact questions with your stakeholders, discuss the appropriate level of evaluation. Do we need to do an impact analysis? Will it be acceptable to show correlational relationships? Remember, the end purpose is making the best decisions you can with the data and resources you have. Information serves to reduce the risk involved in making decisions. If there are great legal or financial consequences, then you should at least consider a more rigorous approach. What information do you and your stakeholders need to make smart decisions and build a winning organization? If you are in a numbers-driven, analytical business culture, it's probably safe to assume that you shouldn't be presenting vanity metrics and correlated relationships in high-stakes business decisions. On the other hand, perhaps you have a low-stakes investment, but a certain stakeholder wants to know how it's performing. Showing a relationship between the investment and results may be more appropriate in such a situation.

What is "Big Data"?

As a strategic leader, you need to be aware of current trends and the fundamentals. You don't always need to understand the details, but you do need to not be blindsided when the topic arises. Big data is typically used in the world of predictive analytics. It essentially means that you analyze all kinds of data from various sources to predict future events. You maximize the amount of information you have to yield the most precise insights. The more data you have about something, the better you can predict its future performance. In your business you may hear references to big data or disparate data, which simply means data are captured from multiple sources.

Update Your Impact Blueprint

After you've analyzed your data and answered your business impact questions, it's time to update your Blueprint. You can color code it to provide a big-picture snapshot of the business impact. Here is the update from the sales representative training example.

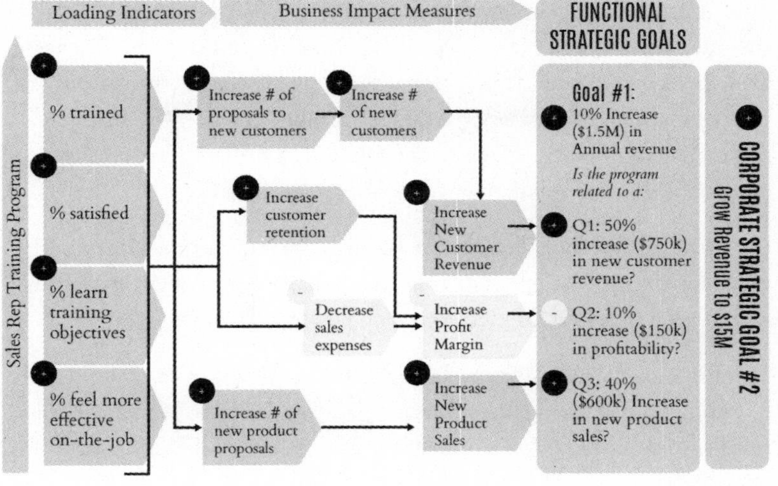

Figure 9.2

In this example, at the end of the year we compared the performance of a group who received the sales training and a similar group of sales representatives who weren't trained yet. For those who took the training, starting at the left, we see that we had some positive (+) activities and output from those who participated in the training. Now, when we look at leading indicators, we see that the trained group brought in more new customers, improved customer retention, and put out more proposals that included the new products. That's great news! However, the trained group had a smaller decrease in sales expenses than the untrained group (-). In terms of business impact, our trained group significantly out-performed the untrained group in increasing our new customer revenue (+) and in increasing new product sales (+). Overall, though, the trained group did not significantly impact the targeted increase in profitability because they didn't have a significant decrease in sales expenses (-), even though they had strong customer retention (+). At the end of the year, the sales rep training was associated with an overall 10.3% increase in annual revenue for the sales function, which was slightly higher than the targeted 10%. This 10.3% increase in revenue helped to meet and exceed the corporate goal to grow revenue to $15 million.

Decision status: Continue to track the data and explore why there isn't a significant decrease in sales expenses in the trained group.

Was it due to a missing component in the training program? Did the sales manager fail to reinforce the issue related to sales expenses? Did the sales reps determine that a reduction in their expenses wasn't as much of a priority when it came to acquiring more new customers and selling more new products in order to hit their goals and the corporate goal?

If strong overall business impact trends continue for another quarter, consider rolling the program out to another region and continuing to monitor results before rolling it out company-wide.

When you're looking at the Impact Blueprint with the metrics in place, you will see that you have proved or disproved some of your assumptions. Now you can look back and make decisions about what to do. The outcome of the Blueprint is that you make decisions about how to change, or depending on your role, recommend changes with data at your back.

Quick and Dirty Takeaways for Factor 5

Here are the highlights to keep in mind as you execute like a strategic leader:

- **As much as you're driving change, change is also happening to you.** Don't be so tied to your plan that you can't pivot when circumstances dictate a new direction.
- **Be aware of everything around you.** Don't operate in the vacuum of your function. Rely on your governance board, stakeholders, and team members to help you understand what's unfolding in real time.
- **You need a winning team to win.** Alternately recognize and redirect your team members for optimal results.
- **Recommend changes in a smart, understandable, and data-driven way.** Understand your audience and use the communication strategies in chapter 3 to make sure your recommendations can be turned into action.
- **Analytic approaches tend to offer more information in exchange for greater efforts and resources.** When you plan for data analysis, make an assessment of what you need to know to make a decision and what level of rigor the culture of your business will require.

Checklist for Factor 5: Execute Your Strategic Plan

- ☐ Have you put your Impact Blueprint into action?
- ☐ Are you monitoring what's happening around you?
- ☐ Do you need to make changes based on the activities you're monitoring in order to achieve your goals?
- ☐ Are you flexible when urgent situations or new, better ideas arise?
- ☐ Do you make decisions based on their fit with the established direction?
- ☐ Have you created a high-functioning and motivated team?
- ☐ Do you understand the basic categories of evaluation and the value of the information you gain by using them?

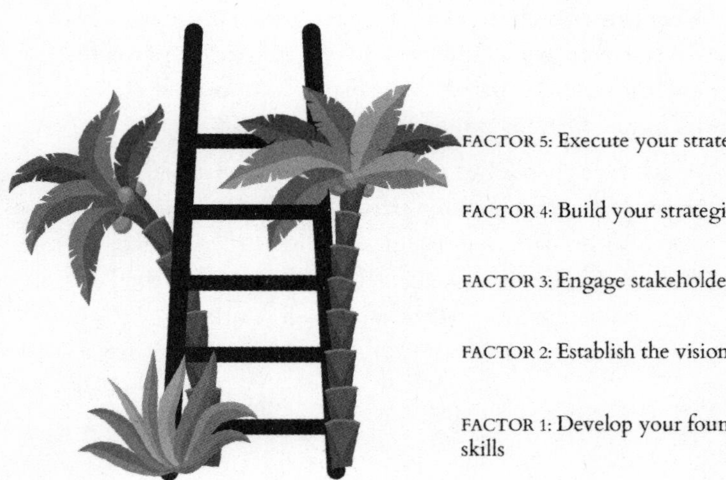

Figure 9.3

Chapter 10

Factor 6—Make Decisions to Win

As a strategic leader, you constantly evaluate what you, your team, your department, and your business are doing. You seek insights into areas where your plan isn't driving the business goals so that you can adjust as quickly and efficiently as possible. In that process, you gain information that allows you to make decisions and drive change. You use that information to alter the plan as needed, but depending on your role in the organization, you may or may not be making those decisions alone. If you make recommendations to a leadership team, those recommendations become powerful because they're backed with data. Recommendations can be fraught with a political overtone, so when you make them, be savvy about what and how you present. If you recommend downsizing or cutting a pet project without adequate supporting data, you may pay for it politically. On the other hand, if you do not recommend cutting a poorly performing program when you have data that suggest it should be cut, you can eventually pay for that, too. An all-too-common reaction to recommended change is that it threatens stability, makes things uncomfortable, and jeopardizes political standings.

Where possible, engage your stakeholders when making significant recommendations. Share your data with them and get their feedback. Giving options can also ease tension—by offering alternate scenarios, you stimulate discussion and debate, and you also give your listener a chance to feel a sense of ownership of the recommendation. Above all, be timely and realistic. If the decision is attached to a certain schedule, don't miss the window of opportunity to share it!

As far as how you deliver a recommendation, here are some tips for making yours more persuasive:

- **Know your audience.** Refer back to the communication strategies in chapter 3. They will help you to ensure you're speaking your audience's language and sharing recommendations in a way that's engaging and appropriate.
- **Communicate with the appropriate person or entity.** If you've found a way to save costs by switching office cleaning crews, do you really need to take that to the CEO? No, you go to the office manager who holds the

contract with the current cleaning company. Figure out who has a vested interest in the changes you're proposing, and also who has the practical responsibility of carrying out the change. Depending on the size and structure of your organization, you may also need to work with power brokers and influencers. Follow the chain of command and figure out where and how you fit in.

- **Make recommendations that are specific and actionable.** If you say, "We need to make our manufacturing process more efficient," you aren't giving anyone anything concrete to go out and do. Instead say, "We can gain manufacturing efficiencies by changing our agreement with our logistics provider to ensure that all the necessary parts are in the factory at least a day in advance of when they're needed." Now the involved parties have something to work with. If you don't know how to make manufacturing more efficient, then the onus is on you to come up with a way to fill that need, and you aren't ready to make a recommendation yet.
- **Focus on a single issue or topic at a time.** Don't muddy the waters by trying to solve several things in one fell swoop. Recommendations with multiple pieces run the risk of being misinterpreted, or critical pieces may be ignored. Help your audience to focus on the most important issue at hand, and then build from there. It's okay to give multiple recommendations, as long as each one is clear and actionable. Ensure your audience is following along with you and isn't confusing your intent. Again, refer back to chapter 3's communication strategies.
- **Don't default to asking for increased funding or resources for a project.** It's fairly obvious that most good programs can be enhanced by a bigger budget, but more money (or an increase in another resource) typically isn't easy to come by. Focus on showing how the existing resources can be reallocated to improve the

impact. That said, if a program has been wildly successful and additional funding is necessary for survival, build your case around the successful track record and include profitable projections.

- **Don't focus on trivial or obvious changes.** Save your political capital for the items that will be a harder sell. Again, this comes back to knowing your audience. If a change is trivial or obvious but you still need to push it through, take it to the appropriate party.
- **Include potential costs, benefits, and barriers to implementing the change.** After you've captured your audience's attention with your recommendation, be sure to engage them on the positive and negative consequences. Emphasis on *after* you've engaged the audience!

  For example:

  We're ready to start selling SuperPuffs to grocers in the tristate area. It will take some time, and we're going up against more competitors by taking this approach so early on, but we have a lot of momentum going right now from our regional tasting events, and as we speak PuffySnack is popping up everywhere. Our product is healthier than theirs, but we need consumers to get that concept before they're hooked on PuffySnack. So there's going to need to be a marketing campaign offering some great deals on SuperPuffs to get more people familiar with the brand that goes along with a tristate launch. But if we can pull all that off, we'll be ready to go nationwide!

  Whoa. There's a lot packed into that recommendation. It's all important information, but it's presented in one long stream of consciousness that is a lot for anybody to digest. Instead, make the initial recommendation, allow the listener to follow up with questions, and work the critical details into the dialogue.

— Coming off the success of our regional tasting events, the next step is to launch SuperPuffs to grocers in the tristate area.

— Really? Don't we run the risk of being overrun by PuffySnack this early on?

— We do, which is exactly why we need to get SuperPuffs out there now. If we wait much longer, consumers will be hooked on PuffySnack and will be less likely to convert to our healthier alternative.

— Hmm, that's a good point. Okay, how do we get this going?

— First, we need to put together a marketing campaign to spread awareness of our brand throughout the tristate area, and along with that offer some great deals for new customers.

It's not just that the second example is easier for the listener to absorb. It's also more collaborative, which helps you gain buy-in from the individual you're trying to convince.

What Happens When You Stumble?

If you're going to be a leader, you're going to make mistakes. Because you're evaluating what you're doing, your mistakes are going to be highlighted, sometimes in a very public way. The worst thing you can do is to ignore them. Sometimes you execute perfectly, but you don't impact the metrics you thought you would, and you still don't meet the goal. Ask yourself:

- Was the original impact theory which comprised your Impact Blueprint wrong?
- Did you impact an unexpected goal?
- Do you need to change something in the way you executed?

In order to win, you absolutely have to be self-aware. How can you improve and keep doing better? Poor outcomes don't automatically mean you're not winning; they indicate a need to step back down your ladder, figure out what happened, learn how to do better, and get back up to the top. The way you lose is by ignoring or attempting to hide the poor outcomes. Also, remember the third rung of your ladder. By engaging your stakeholders and creating a shared culture of accountability, you're all in this together. You all misjudged, and you all have to take steps to fix it. You are the ultimate accountable leader, so galvanize your troops and make the necessary changes. More often than not, if you've built your ladder with authentic rungs, then your missteps can be repaired with tweaks. If a major overhaul is required, it's usually the result of some radical shift in the outside world that you didn't—or couldn't—anticipate. Reserve the right to get smarter as new information comes to you.

Do you know why we chose a ladder as the overarching metaphor for this book? You build your ladder, you climb up it, and you think you've arrived. You're at the top of the jungle, looking out over the trees and seeing the big picture. Congratulations. Now you have to figure out how to stay up there. Ladders wobble, the ground can shift, and the tree your ladder is leaning against can collapse. And don't forget—trees grow! As your organization or department grows, you will continually need to reevaluate your big picture. Is everyone still aligned to the vision and mission?

No matter who you are and what leadership position you find yourself inhabiting, it never gets easy. You don't get to kick back and watch the function, company, government, or organization run itself. People will look to you for active leadership, smart decisions, and answers to the hard questions they don't know how to solve. You can't expect to sit at the top and keep doing the same things you did while you were building the ladder. You're responsible for a bigger component of the business, or maybe the whole business! The decisions you make have higher stakes. It's harder to see what's right and what's wrong, and people are looking to you to set a direction that they will follow. You tend to have fewer facts, more chaos, and less time to ponder. Things that used to seem black and white become gray, because you realize that no one has made the overarching decision above you for you to follow through on. Meanwhile, everyone is looking up at you. Your integrity is at stake in every action. The fate of the business rests on your shoulders.

If you've been working through each factor in this book, you've built yourself a solid foundation in strategic leadership. You're ready to go out there and do it—maybe you already are doing it. The last piece of advice we want you to walk away with is this: *never stop growing*. There is always more to learn about, and just when you think there isn't, the whole world changes and you find yourself in new territory. We recommend striving to set aside ten percent of your time for your own continuing education and improvement. Read books, take classes, attend conferences, use your strategic "think" time, participate in stimulating discussions, connect to your customers, and keep doing the things you learned about in chapter 2, when you were just starting your strategic leadership journey. Understanding the big picture isn't a onetime thing, because the big picture isn't static. Keep updating the picture other leaders have of you—don't give the impression that you've peaked and are on a long slide into retirement.

In addition to the suggestions for understanding the big picture in chapter 2, we have some additional ideas to help you stay at the top.

Apply for industry awards. Awards applications are an excellent learning opportunity because they typically force you to dive deep into what you're doing. You may feel like your work isn't ready for that level of examination, or like you have a long way to go before you would consider putting your group out there. Apply anyway! You may not place, but with most awards programs, you'll receive valuable feedback on what you're doing and how you compare to your peers. Even the process of completing an award application can be a useful opportunity for reflection.

Be a futurist. Where will you be in five years? How do you think the world will evolve? How will your country evolve? How will your industry evolve? How will your organization evolve? Always be thinking about these questions as you plan, make decisions, and survey the jungle. Read and listen to what others have to say on these topics. Invite a professional futurist to speak to your team.

Have a technology plan. Consider your technology landscape today. Where does it need to go in the next few years? Build that into your larger plans. If you aren't in IT, look for ways that you and IT can support and advocate for each other.

Keep the lights on. Depending on your function's maturity, the biggest portion of your annual budget may be continuing to do all the stuff that was already set into motion at some point in the past. You can look for ways to simplify and streamline by cutting this budget back, but you can't ignore it. If you are struggling to keep your strategic vision alive, take a hard look at your ongoing costs for opportunities to free up some resources.

Care for yourself. We talked about this earlier in the book, but it bears repeating here, because it can be easy to neglect your personal needs when you're looking out over the jungle. Don't forget to eat well, exercise, sleep, and take time to relax and recover.

> **Diana**
> Early on as an executive, I crossed paths with Jack Groppel, author of *The Corporate Athlete*. I loved the way he talked about how leaders need to take on the mindset of being a corporate athlete and living by some of the same principles sports athletes do—focusing in on nutrition, fitness, proper sleep, and self-improvement. You have to take care of your mental, physical, and emotional states so you have the energy and ability to perform to truly lead yourself and others to winning results. This is something I am very passionate about and that I live by. I know that I show up as my best self and provide my clients with the best coaching when I exercise, sleep, and eat right. Make the time for yourself! Yes, life will happen, and you can get off of some of your healthy routines, but have a plan and get back on track.

Quick and Dirty Takeaways for Factor 6

Here are the highlights to keep in mind as you execute like a strategic leader:

- **Remember your strategic communication style when making recommendations.** Share data and findings in a way that is actionable and shows your accountability and transparency.
- **Anything can change—be as ready as possible to respond quickly.** Use all six rungs of the ladder to help you make adjustments and respond when you make mistakes.
- **Come back to the first rung of the ladder as you create your ongoing development plan.** Never stop learning and growing.

Checklist for Factor 6: Make Decisions to Win

- ☐ Are you doing the things necessary to stay sharp, relevant, and at the top of your field?
- ☐ Are you sharing findings and using information to drive meaningful change?
- ☐ Can you see over the trees to make sure your team is in the right jungle?

Figure 10.1

Conclusion

As we wrap up this book and send you out into the world to be more strategic, we wanted to leave you with a final note of encouragement to go out there and make it happen! Don't be afraid to take risks in your career—things may not go the way you hope they will, but chances are those risks will have a positive impact over the long run. Create your vision and go after it!

We've given you a lot of things to think about and apply to help you become a more strategic leader who can achieve and sustain winning results. We encourage you to review the checklists at the end of each chapter, which we've compiled here for you.

Factor 1: Develop your foundational skills

- ☐ Do you understand the big picture of your organization, as well as your place in it?
- ☐ Are you knowledgeable about what's going on inside and outside of your organization?
- ☐ Do you set time aside for strategic thinking?
- ☐ Do you have the executive presence of a strategic leader?
- ☐ Are you accountable for your actions?
- ☐ Does your calendar work for you?
- ☐ Do you have a vision for your career and life?
- ☐ Do you have a personal development board of stakeholders committed to your success?
- ☐ Are you communicating like a strategic leader by connecting to your audience, thinking about your messaging, and sharing the right amount of detail?
- ☐ Do you listen with the intent to hear, with an understanding of both words and body language?

Factor 2: Establish the vision

- ☐ Have you created a well-defined vision and strategy for your function?
- ☐ Are your function's vision and strategy aligned to the broader organization's vision and strategy?
- ☐ Is your strategy concrete and measurable?
- ☐ Does everyone on your team understand the vision and current strategy, and is each team member able to explain them?
- ☐ Does everyone on your team know how their work aligns to the business and higher vision?

Factor 3: Engage stakeholders

- ☐ Have you built a functional governance board of stakeholders to help guide and support your work?
- ☐ Are your stakeholders looking across the organization to help you see the opportunities and anticipate challenges?
- ☐ Have you fostered a culture of accountability on your governance board?

Factor 4: Build your strategic plan

- ☐ Are you following the Plan, Do, Study, Act model?
- ☐ Do you have a list of business impact questions that will provide what you need to know in order to continuously win?
- ☐ Have you created an inventory of your enablers?
- ☐ Have you created an Impact Blueprint that is vetted and supported by your stakeholders?
- ☐ Are you using leading indicators of business impact and business impact measures appropriately, making decisions within the context of the right jungle?

Factor 5: Execute your strategic plan

- ☐ Have you put your Impact Blueprint into action?
- ☐ Are you monitoring what's happening around you?
- ☐ Do you need to make changes based on the activities you're monitoring in order to achieve your goals?
- ☐ Are you flexible when urgent situations or new, better ideas arise?
- ☐ Do you make decisions based on their fit with the established direction?
- ☐ Have you created a high-functioning and motivated team?
- ☐ Do you understand the basic categories of evaluation and the value of the information you gain by using them?

Factor 6: Make decisions to win

- ☐ Are you doing the things necessary to stay sharp, relevant, and at the top of your field?
- ☐ Are you sharing findings and using information to drive meaningful change?
- ☐ Can you see over the trees in order to make sure your team is in the right jungle?

Remember to always keep growing and learning. The best leaders are the best learners, and they surround themselves with the brightest and most productive people. You picked up and read this book because you wanted to grow, so congratulations, keep growing! Identify someone you trust to help give you the feedback you need to grow—such as the people on your personal development board. Alternatively, you can always look outside your organization for a coach. Even if your company doesn't require it, have a current self-development plan in place that continues to stretch you, and make time in your calendar for your learner role. Remember to take a strategic approach to your development: Revisit the company's vision, its strategic goals, and your functional goals, and determine if there are behaviors you need to demonstrate at a higher level to better assist in execution. And of course, have and achieve measurable goals tied to the business so you can show your impact.

Diana

In addition to what is in the book, here are a few things I coach executive and up-and-coming leaders to do:

1. Identify any derailing or distracting behaviors that would prevent you from moving up the corporate ladder or landing your ideal position. After talking with a few of my clients' coworkers, bosses, and employees, it's usually easy to identify whether there are derailing factors. Then work on stopping those things that will hold you back from being successful or prevent others from supporting you.

2. Become familiar with and strive to acquire and demonstrate the competencies and behaviors other leaders are demonstrating when they've reached the level you want to achieve. In addition to the checklists we've created, review your company's leadership competencies. If they don't have any established, reread the leadership competencies and behaviors we included in chapter 1. Spend time with the successful leaders in your organization, maybe even shadowing them for a day. Develop and implement a plan to fill your leadership gaps.

3. Continue to check in with your stakeholders to see if you are making the progress needed to be more strategic and adjust accordingly.

We hope you learn from the lessons we have shared with you. If we knew then what we know now, we would have succeeded at a higher level in our former positions. Here are two final stories about risks we took early in our careers, and the lessons we learned along the way.

Diana

When I first moved from an operations role to McDonald's corporate human resources, I felt really out of my element. My knowledge and skills were based in the restaurants. That was how I had proven my leadership to that point, but succeeding in corporate required a completely different skill set. One of my responsibilities in my first HR role was to field phone calls from employees who were contacting HR with questions or issues. Every time I picked up that phone, I felt anxious. What would the caller ask? Would I understand the nuances of the question? Would I have the right answer? I desperately wanted to be supportive and helpful. What I quickly realized was the way to truly help people was to stay focused on helping customers (both internal and external) and tap into the resources around me. I didn't need to have all the answers, and I didn't have to try to pretend that I was a fount of knowledge on the phone. I began to see that my responsibility was to track down the right answer. With that shift in focus, I felt less afraid to pick up the phone and more empowered to do my new corporate job. And there, at the bottom of the corporate ladder, I learned two important lessons that I carried with me as a leader, even to the VP level: truly care about your customers—especially when supporting those who support the paying customers—and that I didn't need to have all the answers in my own brain. I did need to surround myself with people who could help me find the right answers.

Stacey

Early in my career, I was an evaluator for an e-learning company, working on projects in the research department. I loved my job, but I felt pigeonholed in my cube crunching data all day. The extrovert in me was ready to get out and make a visible impact. I didn't really have a big picture of what the company did or what it was trying to accomplish, but I was curious about all of that. Keep in mind that this was on the cusp of the internet, so a lot of information wasn't publicly available. I did network, but that only got me so far. I was perceived as the PhD with good Excel skills. I decided that if I wanted to gain insight at the executive level without going around my manager, the chief learning officer, I had to find a way onto a corporate strategic project.

I heard that the president of the company wanted to build a balanced scorecard to measure how well the different departments were executing against the corporate strategy. I immediately thought, bingo! That's the project I want and need. I went to my boss and told him that I thought I was the best person to spearhead the scorecard project because of my measurement background. Honestly, I wasn't sure what a balanced scorecard was at the time, nor did I know much about formal business strategy, but I knew that I was smart enough and quick enough to figure it out, or at least make it look like I knew what I was doing while I overcame my learning curve on the back end. My boss advocated for me, and I landed on the executive team to build the corporate scorecard. That project got me into the C-suite; I was soon known by all departments and was recognized even higher in our parent organization when I was asked to build the scorecard for the parent company. I was now seen as someone who was good at more than Excel. Over time, the insights I gained through the scorecard project allowed me to create the niche where I built my career, and also to move quickly into executive positions with other firms. My career path was firmly set because I went after a strategic project for which no one would've considered me at the time. I learned that I needed to be proactive in the business world and seek out my own opportunities.

We wish you all the best!

Be In Touch

You're building your own ladder in the jungle, and we want to hear about it! How have you applied the six factors for strategic leadership? What new opportunities have you seized? We would love to hear from you. Please reach out to us on our website, *www.bemorestrategicinbusiness.com*, or by visiting the social media pages for Be More Strategic in Business.

We speak regularly at leadership, learning, and human resources events. Visit *bemorestrategicinbusiness.com/speaking* to book Diana and/or Stacey for your next event.

You can also work closely with Diana or Stacey on any of the six factors by booking a coaching or consulting engagement. To receive one-on-one leadership coaching and mentoring from Diana, visit *www.winning-results-llc.com*. To consult with Stacey on evaluating investments, connecting to business results, and building an Impact Blueprint for your organization, visit *www.smarterpeopleplanning.com*.

Acknowledgements

First and foremost, we would like to acknowledge the incredible partnership and guidance provided by our writer and editor, Sara Jensen. Sara was the connecting beam of the A-frame construction that built this book. Scott Miller and Annie Oswald at Franklin Covey provided invaluable coaching, and we were honored by Stephen M.R. Covey's foreword. Jenny Garner's expertise enhanced our communication content. Hugo Villabona and the rest of the Mango Publishing team successfully brought our vision to fruition. Finally, a special thank you to the winning leaders who believed in this project enough to give us feedback and add their credibility.

Diana

Thank you foremost to Jerry, my incredible husband, best friend, and life partner. Without his support and partnership, I wouldn't be the person I am today. Thank you to my two amazing daughters, Kirsten Marie Elizabeth and Jena Nicole, who traveled, moved, and supported me throughout my career and from whom I continue to learn so much. I am incredibly proud of the strong, smart and caring women they have grown into and love the men they have brought into our family, Evan and Will.

I am so grateful to my parents for the strong foundation they gave me—Edgar Glenn, who told me and made me believe I could be and do anything I wanted. To my mom Sam, who showed me by her example that you can have your desired career and a loving family and still make time for yoga and continue to be an avid learner. Thank you to my siblings, Tricia, Bobby, and Karen, as well as our extended family that has supported me along the way.

A big thank you to my awesome team members that made being a leader so much fun, so rewarding, and an incredible growth opportunity.

Finally, to my partner Stacey, who co-supported the vision and strategy of developing a practical book that could help leaders become more strategic and make better decisions, thank you! You balance out my style, truly helping us create a winning team dedicated to helping other leaders.

Stacey

I would like to thank my former and future employers, clients, managers, mentors, colleagues, employees, professors, and other leaders who gave me the opportunity to develop stronger leadership under their watch.

I thank my mom, Mary, for supporting me as I flourish and thrive. Leisa, my sister, is my kindred spirit, whose own growth and success is awe-inspiring. My brother Alex's work ethic and ability to reinvent reminds me every day of life's rewards. John Nelsons' belief in me and ongoing wisdom gives me continuous confidence. Beverly and Lyle have been an inspiration for my lifelong drive. Tony and Bob always bring joy to my heart and laughter to my day. Linda Boyle's unconditional love grounds me, and I cherish Michael Boyle's longtime friendship. Sayge, Kayla, Nora, and Maddox give me immense pride and faith in the future. Linda Biggs, my BFF, has been my unwavering sounding board and fitness partner throughout this process, and Jim Biggs' inspirational words energize me.

Diana Thomas is my strategic leader role model. I will never stop learning from and being inspired by her. Our journey together is immensely rewarding and enables me to see the world more strategically. Thank you for making me a stronger leader and for believing in what we can accomplish together.

Recommended Reading

Looking for more? This is a brief selection of books that have influenced our professional and personal development throughout our careers and inspired parts of this book.

The 4 Disciplines of Execution: Achieving Your Wildly Important Goals. Sean Covey, Chris McChesney, and Jim Huling (2016)

Big Data: A Revolution That Will Transform How We Live, Work, and Think. Viktor Mayer-Schoenberger and Kenneth Cukier (2013)

The Corporate Athlete: How to Achieve Maximal Performance in Business and Life. Jack Groppel (1999)

Crucial Conversations: Tools for Talking When the Stakes Are High. Kerry Patterson and Joseph Grenny (2011)

Difficult Conversations: How to Discuss What Matters Most. Douglas Stone, Bruce Patton, and Sheila Heen (1999)

How to Measure Anything: Finding the Value of Intangibles in Business. Douglas W. Hubbard (2014)

How to Win Friends and Influence People in the Digital Age. Dale Carnegie & Associates (2011)

Keeping Up with the Quants: Your Guide to Understanding and Using Analytics. Thomas H. Davenport and Jinho Kim (2013)

Lean In: Women, Work, and the Will to Lead. Sheryl Sandberg (2013)

Superforecasting: The Art and Science of Prediction. Philip E. Tetlock and Dan Gardner (2015)

Talking from 9 to 5: Women and Men at Work. Deborah Tannen (2001)

The Leadership Challenge James M. Kouzes and Barry Z. Posner (2017)

Triggers: Creating behavior that lasts—Becoming the person you want to be. Marshall Goldsmith and Mark Reiter (2015)

Verbal Judo: The Gentle Art of Persuasion. George J. Thompson and Jerry B. Jenkins (2013)

What Got You Here Won't Get You There. Marshall Goldsmith (2007)

About the Authors

Diana Thomas

Diana Thomas is an executive coach who partners with business executives, teams, and learning leaders to help them become more strategic and find more happiness in their lives. She brings deep expertise from her career as U.S. Vice President for Learning and Development at McDonald's Corporation, where she led all aspects of training and development at Hamburger University, McDonald's global training center of excellence. Her work there was recognized with numerous learning industry awards. Today she uses her decades of experience, education, and expertise to help her clients increase their organizational impact and grow a committed and engaged followership. She is an editorial advisory board member for Chief Learning Officer magazine, a faculty member for MediaTec's CLO Accelerator, and board member for the National Diversity Council.

Stacey Boyle

Dr. Stacey Boyle has led global consulting and research departments for over twenty years, during which time she has built a reputation for groundbreaking work connecting investments in people to critical business outcomes. Today she runs Smarter People Planning, a consultancy that helps some of the world's top companies and nonprofits answer their pressing business questions and make strategic decisions. Stacey is a sought-after thought leader in workforce analytics, evaluation, and management consulting. Her experience spans across a wide variety of industries, including the learning industry's most popular service providers and awards programs. She holds a PhD in Applied Behavioral Research and Evaluation from Oklahoma State University.

TRUSSVILLE PUBLIC LIBRARY
201 PARKWAY DRIVE
TRUSSVILLE, AL 35173
(205) 655-2022